PACE CARS of the INDY 500®

L. Spencer Riggs

SPEED AGE® INC.
Publisher
Fort Lauderdale, Florida

FIRST EDITION

Library of Congress Catalog Number 89-091600

ISBN: 0-9622805-0-X

For Information:
Speed Age Inc.
P.O. Box 7373, Ft. Lauderdale, FL 33338

PRINTED IN THE UNITED STATES OF AMERICA

Acknowledgements

Editor: Linda K. Luedecke

Photo Coordination: Ron McQueeney

Dust Cover Artist: Henry Imms

Production Coordinator: Kenneth B. Luedecke

Graphics and Typography: Wendy A. Abernethy

Photos Furnished By: Indianapolis Motor Speedway Corporation

Printed By: Lithotone, Inc./Elkhart, Indiana

Many interesting facts were gleaned from dozens of personal collections and memorabilia, filed away—seemingly unimportant—awaiting our search. The list is too numerous to mention each and everyone. A tremendous thanks to one and all.

The author would like to thank the following individuals and organizations for their valuable assistance.

Kim Miller librarian of the ANTIQUE AUTO CLUB of AMERICA; Ron Grantz curator of the NATIONAL AUTOMOTIVE HISTORY COLLECTION, DETROIT PUBLIC LIBRARY; Randy Mason HENRY FORD MUSEUM; Skip Marketti and Lee Beck AUBURN CORD MUSEUM; Thomas Appel STUDEBAKER MUSEUM; INDIANAPOLIS PUBLIC LIBRARY; SPEEDWAY CITY PUBLIC LIBRARY.

Randy Fox of PONTIAC; Hellen Jones Earley OLDSMOBILE HISTORY CENTER and Laura Joseph of OLDSMOBILE ENGINEERING & FACTS CENTER; Dave Hederich of CHEVROLET; Lawrence R. Gustin of BUICK; Bruce R. Thomas, T.W. Jakobowski and Phil Bockhorn of CHRYSLER; Mr. Glen S. Lyall of FORD.

In addition, the author would like to thank the following. Without their cooperation, patience and perseverance, the production of this book would have been impossible.

Mrs. Floyd Davis; Merlene Potts; Ron McQueeney of INDIANAPOLIS 500 PHOTOGRAPHY; Jack L. Martin; Joseph J. Cole; Sam Hanks, Duke Nalon; Hal Robson; Mauri Rose, Jr.; Eldon Palmer; and the late Ted Everroade.

A special debt of thanks to Ken Luedecke and the staff of SPEED AGE PUBLISHING for their unending support; and to William R. Donaldson, Director of Marketing, Indianapolis Motor Speedway Corp.

Last, but not least, a warm thank you to my wife, Judy, son Joseph Riggs, daughter Ella I. Riggs and my mother Ella A. Riggs—who kept the coffee pot on. Thank you for not letting me give up.

L. Spencer Riggs

PREFACE

It is not recorded when or where the first pacemaker—or in latter day parlance, pace car—came into being*. It appears that as early as 1907 or '08, the Brooklands race course in Surrey, England, may have made the first use of a pacemaking vehicle. Colonel Lindsay Lloyd, the Clerk of the Course, (Chief Steward) was often photographed at the wheel of a Rolls-Royce or Bentley, leading, or about to do so, a field of racers round Brooklands.

In the United States, there seems little doubt the Indianapolis Motor Speedway made the first use of a pacemaking vehicle.

There may be claims to the contrary. Perhaps even valid ones. The two examples given, however, appear to be the most recognized. One reason is, both racing venues were among the first to use a "rolling start" at their events.

The pacemaker came into being, in order that anxious drivers might have their speed held in check at a uniform pace. Otherwise, and in many instances in those halcyon days of yore, races sometimes "started" long before the starter's flag dropped. The pacemaker kept down the squabbling, accidents and promoted safety on the course.

Throughout the years, Indy Pace Cars have enjoyed the most prestigious position of any "passenger cars" in the world. Very early on, various moguls of the automotive world, realized the advantage of having their products lead the fastest 33 cars on earth, over the speedway's starting line.

The position of Indy Pace Car has been known to alter the course of faltering marques, and with it, the fortunes of some of the Twentieth Century's best known captains of industry.

Many people ask how an Indy Pace Car is selected. Over the decades, the actual process has changed surprisingly little, since speedway president Carl G. Fisher used his own Stoddard-Dayton passenger car to pace the 1911 race.

The Stoddard-Dayton had established an amazing record in racing. In 1909, Lewis Schwitzer, driving an S-D, won the first race of any kind held at the Indianapolis Motor Speedway.

Today, the various chief officials of the Indianapolis Motor Speedway Corporation still choose a pace car by performance and outstanding new designs in styling and engineering. As with our latest pace car, the 1989 Pontiac Trans Am, a commemorative anniversary of a marque, may enter into the selection process. This is essentially the same prerequisites set down by speedway founders Fisher, Arthur Newby, Frank Wheeler and James Allison in the very beginning.

As a native of Indianapolis, the author always looks forward to the announcement of the pace car selection. The heralding of the Indy Pace Car, puts a strong sense of 500 in the air, long before the spine tingling noise, and perfume of racing rents the quiet on West Sixteenth Street. It is the very first sign of preparation for the greatest event in auto racing.

Although the main sources of Indy Pace Cars are now, more or less confined to the big three of Chrysler, Ford and General Motors, the competition to draw the attention of IMS officials is keener now than ever.

With the advent of television coverage beaming the biggest one day sporting event in the world to millions of people around the globe, the pace car selection is considered one of the largest plums in promotional advertising. Not to mention the bragging rights for a year!

Today, most of the different manufacturing divisions instruct their design studios to have a viable pace car idea on the drawing board, should IMS point its finger in their direction and say, "Uncle Indy Wants You!"

A friend of the author, who was in automotive sales, once related that "being selected Indy Pace Car is better than a subliminal advertisement." He qualified this statement by saying, "look how many race fans purchase the same year car as the pacemaker. Also, the average motorist feels the pace car is a cut above the other automobiles on the market."

He was correct, too.

INDIANAPOLIS MOTOR SPEEDWAY

When I took stock, I realized my family had collectively purchased nearly a dozen pace car "same year" models. As a matter-of-fact, the author's first car was a pace car model year. And, at the time of ownership, I wasn't even aware of it!

So, sit back and enjoy a trip through Indy Pace Car history. It's really the history of our automotive industry.

You'll read about the tremendous success and failure. The great, near great and a few lemons.

Engines so advanced, their very nature, cost, or the economic situation of their day, doomed them to failure. Everything from the monstrous 525 cubic inch Stoddard-Daytons and early Packard V-12s, to the jewel-like 135 cubic inch 1987 Chrysler Le Baron, and turbocharged "Super Pace Cars" of the last two decades.

Ford's phenomenal sales of the Mustang, kicked off by a pace lap at Indy, and J.J. Cole's advanced "Aero Eight"—nearly out of business by its turn at Indy—give the reader some idea of the drama sometimes associated with the pace car.

So, after long and exhaustive research, we hope to put you in the driver's seat. You're in the Indy Pace Car. The eleven rows of three are lined up behind you. It's time for "Gentlemen, Start Your Engines." Be our guest—turn the page, and choose your favorite pace car.

Sincerely,
L. Spencer Riggs

*AUTHOR'S NOTE: The original term for pace car was pacemaker or pacesetter. The more modern "pace car", although used as slang for years, came into official usage in 1965. These three terms are universally interchangeable, and do not denote a change in the type of vehicle being described.

DEDICATION

I dedicate this work to the memory of my grandfather Joseph Riggs, my father Ivan Riggs and Ted Everroade—a great friend of the author, and the racing and automotive world in general. It was with their insistence and patience, the author came to know the difference between a true automobile and a mere conveyance.

TABLE OF CONTENTS

STODDARD-DAYTON

1911

1911

If ever a man demonstrated his love for an automobile, it was Indianapolis Motor Speedway founder Carl G. Fisher. His immaculate white Stoddard-Dayton, carrying his monogram initials on its radiator, was a personal trademark. Mr. Fisher owned a Stoddard-Dayton dealership in Indianapolis, and it is widely believed that he was an investor in the firm.

In order to draw attention to his beloved car, Fisher attached a huge gas balloon to an S-D roadster—sans engine—announcing his intention to fly the 1500 pound machine over Indianapolis, as an advertisement. On October 30, 1908, Fisher—no faintheart when it came to daring do—and G.L. Bumbaugh ascended from the Indianapolis Gas Company, flew the Stoddard-Dayton over the city, and landed in Indy's suburb of Southport. The stunt brought even more attention than Fisher had imagined, making nearly every major daily newspaper in the country.

The following year, Fisher was made a distributor-dealer for the state of Indiana.

Fisher decided to use his very own Stoddard-Dayton Model 11-A Touring Car as the first Indianapolis 500-mile race pace car. The very same machine depicted in the famous 1909 photo, showing the speedway president taking some decidely shaken reporters for a high-speed tour of his new track.

This not withstanding, the Stoddard-Dayton, on its own merits, had earned the honor as Indy's first pacemaker. Lewis Schwitzer had piloted a Stoddard-Dayton Model 9-H to victory in the very first race held over the Indianapolis Motor Speedway on August 14, 1909.

The rapid Stoddard-Dayton was the work of brothers John and Charles Stoddard of Dayton, Ohio. The Stoddards had been in the farm machinery business before switching to auto production.

Our pacemaker's engine was an in-line 4-cylinder displacing 251 cubic inches with a bore and stroke of 4 x 5. It was said to develop 35 horsepower. However, this was probably a conservative rating for this highly advanced engine. Designed by a young English engineer, H.J. Edwards, the four-banger was probably the first hemi-head engine produced in America. Edwards designed an intricate series of pushrods and rocker arms to operate the S-D's inclined valves. A push-pull arrangement allowed one rocker to open and close two valves working off a single camshaft located in the crankcase. Powerful expansion springs were used to return the pushrods through the firing cycle. The totally exposed valve train was made of brass, exhibiting superb craftsmanship. The intake and exhaust were siamesed. Each cylinder sported two spark plugs. One set of four fired by battery and coil ignition, until the magneto took over, firing the other four. A racy twin-branch exhaust manifold suggested the sporty performance of the Stoddard-Dayton engine.

Mr. Fisher drove the pacemaker himself.

Due to several early racing fatalities—none of which involved their creations—the Stoddards soon withdrew their cars from competition. Nevertheless, other private entrants continued to race the marque—perhaps one of the fastest early day cars in America.

Carl Fisher drives the Stoddard-Dayton.

STUTZ

1912

1912

Harry Clayton Stutz was certainly the Horatio Alger of the auto industry. Born June 12, 1876, on a farm near Ansonia, Ohio, young Harry gave evidence of his talents at an early age. In 1898, he put a machine together from cast-off farm equipment. No one realized it then, but the ungainly contraption dubbed "Old Hickory," was the forerunner of a line of great automobiles.

By 1911, Stutz was headquartered in Indianapolis. That year, a Stutz racer—not much more than stock—driven by Gil Anderson, finished eleventh in the inaugural Indianapolis 500-mile race. A jubilant Harry proclaimed his creation "the car that made good in a day."

Harry had driven in a few races, and knew from experience how the public warmed to any automotive product connected with racing. The following year, he built a team of racers that scorched the tracks of America, winning 25 of 28 events.

When the speedway president, Carl G. Fisher, approached Stutz with the idea of his car pacing the 1912 Indianapolis 500, the publicity conscious Harry jumped at the idea. Fisher explained the pace car would be chosen every year, becoming a traditional part of the great race.

Other people had other ideas, however, and the pace car idea almost ended in this, the second year of the Indianapolis 500-mile race.

After a disagreement with Fisher over the condition of the track, starter Fred J. Wagner broke the startling news at a driver's meeting the night of May 27. "There will be no pace car to lead the field on race day," Wagner announced. "Select yourselves someone from the front row to act as your pacemaker." Gil Anderson and Ralph DePalma tied in the voting.

When Fisher was informed of the incident the following morning, he went right over Wagner's head to superior AAA officials. The matter was dropped, and Fisher, accompanied by C.W. Stoddard, pulled the Stutz two-seater roadster to the head of the field.

Without Fisher's tough stand, the Indianapolis 500 might not have a pace car today.

The 4-cylinder Stutz pace car possessed bore and stoke dimensions of $4\frac{3}{4}$ x $5\frac{1}{2}$ which measured out to 290 cubic inches. The Wisconsin-built T-head engine cranked over at 1500 rpm was rated at 60 horsepower. It was a direct development of the Stutz competition model, complete with dual ignition, high pressure lubrication and a Schebler carburetor. It carried ten-spoke wheels on the front, twelve-spoke on the rear, mounting 4.75 x 5.5 inch tires.

In the race, Charles Merz drove a Stutz to fourth place, giving the marque an even grander image, proving their rugged dependablity.

Stutz sales rose from 759 cars in 1913, to 2207 in 1917.

Harry Stutz was ahead of his time with much of his thinking. He envisioned America's interest in sports cars four decades before the two-seater European imports became popular. His Stutz Bearcat was already geared to that market in 1913.

He designed a rear axle with transmission and differential gears all in one unit. The idea was very similar in principle to the modern day transaxle units. From 1911 to '21, all Stutz products—even to their race cars—used this setup.

Like many visionaries, Stutz was not a good money manager. In 1916, he fell prey to Wall Street money lenders, and lost control of the company. In 1919, he left the Stutz organization to start another business.

A Stutz—at least in name—would never again pace the Indianapolis 500.

However, "the greatest race course in the world" had not seen the last of Harry C. Stutz.

6
PRINTING

STODDARD-DAYTON

1913

Even before the first 500-mile race was held, the Stoddard brothers must have felt the larger automotive companies breathing down their necks. In the summer of 1910, in deference to being gobbled up at a loss, they joined Benjamin Brisco's United States Motor Car Company.

Brisco's large conglomerate, made up of Brush, Maxwell, Alden Sampson and other small manufacturers, was designed to do battle with General Motors. This may sound absurd today, but in that era, the S-D and Maxwell lines enjoyed a tremendous following. Unfortunately, this could not be said of the majority of his various cars, and Brisco was not of the same business mold as Bill Durant.

By September of 1912, Brisco's empire had disintegrated. The only division to survive was Maxwell. In early 1913, it was announced that "for the time being" the Stoddard-Dayton Division would produce cars under the auspices of Maxwell.

Therefore, it was hoped the choice of a 139-inch wheelbase two-passenger Stoddard-Dayton roadster as pacemaker for the 500-mile race, would boost the fortunes of the once fabled marque.

Details of this pacemaker are sketchy, but most experts agree it was powered by a 6-cylinder Knight engine. During 1911, Stoddard-Dayton obtained a license to use this highly regarded motor, already the choice of such overseas giants as Daimler, Mercedes, Panhard and Minerva.

The brainchild of Charles Yale Knight, this sleeve valve engine was a story unto itself.

Dubbed the "Silent Knight" by its admirers, this gentle brute produced an amazing 70 horsepower. Since each respective licensee produced the Knight to their own measurements, it is difficult to say, with any certainty, what our pacemaker's exact dimensions were. The figures most often quoted are 525 cubic inches with a bore and stroke of $4\frac{1}{2} \times 5\frac{1}{2}$. The quiet operation was due to the two sleeve per cylinder design, which eliminated the need for the noisy poppet valves of the era. The outer sliding sleeve operated against the cylinder block, while the inner sleeve containing the piston, which in turn was operating within the inner sleeve, slid up and down inside the outer sleeve. Rectangular intake and exhaust ports were cut in the upper end of both sleeves, taking the place of valves. The sleeve walls were 1/8-inch thick, with pin holes and grooves for lubrication. The sleeves were actuated via one-inch connecting rods working on an eccentric shaft, which was operated by a gear on the crankshaft. This took the place of a regular camshaft and valve assembly. There were no valves to float, or get in the way of spark plug replacement. Plugs were placed in the center of the combustion chamber for better breathing, and to retard detonation.

In spite of its complex features, the Knight was a rugged engine. An excellent example of this, was the Mercedes-Knight entry in this very same 1913 Indianapolis 500. Powered by the smallest engine in the race at 250 cubic inches, the Knight was giving up—in some cases—200 cubic inches to its rivals. Nevertheless, the rugged little machine powered the Belgian, Theodore Pilette, to a stunning fifth place finish at 68.15 mph.

Our pacemaker was driven by speedway president Carl G. Fisher.

1913

GRAND STAND
C
17
27
16
19

STODDARD-DAYTON

Benjamin Brisco's well known phrase, "for the time being," translated into only a matter of months for the once renowned Stoddard-Dayton. The company had folded long before the 1914 Indianapolis 500 rolled around.

Not even this could remove the S-D from Carl Fisher's heart. So, for the first and only time in Indianapolis history, a car no longer in production led the starting field to the line.

Undoubtedly, this pacemaker was a 1913 model, updated to what the '14 may have been intended to be. At any rate, there were no 1914 Stoddard-Daytons or Stoddard-Knights produced.

Our pacemaker was powered by the same Knight "double sleeve" engine design as the '13 model.

It is believed the overall concept of these cars remained the handiwork of H.J. Edwards.

Of course, the pace car driver was Carl Fisher. After all, he was the undisputed champion of the Stoddard-Dayton.

Unlike the S-D, Charles Knight and his amazing engine continued on.

Finally, the auto industry made strides in metallurgy, and redesigned the valve principle into the quiet component we know today. The sleeve valve engine slipped grudgingly by the wayside. High costs, high oil consumption and problems with unbalanced reciprocating weight—especially in latter years when higher rev limits became necessary—doomed the remarkable Knight.

But what of Knight the man? The transplanted Hoosier, who built his first engine in Oak Park, Illinois in 1903, and spent so much of his life in England the British thought him their's by birth.

He lived to see his creation turned into powerful V-8 designs, and used in nearly every configuration and application open to an internal combustion engine. He and his engine died the same year—1940. Knight—the man, in Pasadena. Knight—the engine, in Belgium, when Minerva stopped production.

Many historians like to romanticize about the Stoddard-Dayton, pointing out that whatever assets the company left behind were absorbed by the Maxwell Motor Company. In turn, that company was purchsed by Walter P. Chrysler in the early 1920s, and became the Chrysler Corporation. And so, even if once or twice removed, historians contend the descendants of the Stoddard-Dayton live on. And why not? It was a grand old machine.

1914

PACKARD

Since the summer of 1899, when James Ward Packard, his brother William Doud Packard, George L. Weiss and W.A. Hatcher formed the combine that would produce the original Packard motor car, impeccable taste and quality had been their hallmark. The original organization was first called Packard and Weiss, then the Ohio Automobile Company and finally, the Packard Motor Car Company. When the board of directors voted to move to Detroit, from their original home in Warren, Ohio, William Doud Packard decided to stay home to run his lucrative electrical business.

By the time the Indianapolis Motor Speedway chose Packard as the 1915 pace car, the slogan "Ask the Man Who Owns One," was a household phrase. Indeed it's safe to say you'd hear few complaints from Packard owners in that era. Active in racing for many years, Packard quickly accepted the honor, furnishing the speedway with it's latest Model 548.

Our pacemaker was powered by a 525 cubic inch 6-cylinder L-head poppet-valve engine with a bore and stroke of 4½ x 5½ inches. This huge engine developed 60 horsepower at 1720 rpm. Together with the Knight engined Stoddard-Daytons of 1913 and '14, our 1915 Packard shares the distinction of the largest engine in Indy Pace Car history. This motor was sufficient, with huge 37 inch wheels and 3.11 gearing, to haul the heavy 143-inch wheelbase car along at 70 mph. Not surprisingly, with this turn of speed, advertisements of the day proclaimed the Packard "Boss of the Road."

Our pace car driver, for the fifth and last time, was Indianapolis Motor Speedway president Carl G. Fisher. Who could blame Mr. Fisher? The car was from his own Fisher Automobile Company showroom, at 400 North Capitol Avenue!

It was certainly not the last time we would see a Packard lead the Indianapolis starting field over the line.

As a matter-of-fact, Packard had the distinction of pacing one of the few non-500-mile events held over the Indianapolis course.

A Packard roadster, driven by Carl G. Fisher, served as pacemaker for the little remembered "Harvest Racing Classic" held September 9, 1916, at IMS. All three events, consisting of 20, 50 and 100-mile races, were won by Johnny Aitken in a Peugeot. This was the last event held at the Brickyard, prior to World War I.

1915 Packard Six (Photo courtesy Michael Kollins Collection).

PREMIER

1916

With the war in Europe curtailing foreign entries, and prospects for a short field of cars, Indianapolis Motor Speedway officials took two major steps. They cut the race distance to 300-miles. They also asked the Indianapolis based Premier Motor Car Company to produce three racers—virtual copies—of the popular French Peugeots. Premier's new president, Joliet, Illinois banker, F.W. Woodruff, was more than happy to comply. Premier had gone into receivership in 1914, and Premier founder, George B. Weidely, and his partner, Harold Smith, had already left the firm. Plagued by lagging sales, Woodruff hoped the additional public exposure would give the Premier a boost.

Only one of the racers, driven by Gil Anderson, finished the race. This was, however, a creditable seventh.

Whether in return for Woodruff's efforts to bolster the starting field—perhaps in honor of the three racers taking part—Premier's highly regarded 1916 passenger car was selected as pacemaker.

The Model 6-56 was powered by an overhead valve 6-cylinder 403.5 cubic inch engine. This highly refined 4 x 5½ bore and stroker produced 38.4 horsepower. Premier had long since—before many of its prestigious rivals—gone to a progressive sliding gear transmission, and discarded chain for shaft drive.

The handsome 134-inch wheelbase machine, was easily recognized by its streamlined cowl lamps and V-shaped radiator. Much of the design and engineering work came from the hand of the already departed Weidely, however, not much of this is evident on our pacemaker. Apparently, it was stripped down, somewhat. According to photographs, this would appear to be the case.

When pacemaker driver Frank E. Smith led the 21 racers over the line, it was, and remains, to this day, the smallest starting field in Indianapolis 500-mile race history.

Premier went through an almost continual cycle of receivership to new owner, to receivership and another new owner. The end came in October 1926.

Premier laid claim to being the first automotive firm to adopt an emblem—the oak leaf—as a trademark. It seems Premier's only major automotive contribution that survived the firm's demise.

1916

1916 Premier with driver Frank E. Smith behind the wheel.

PACKARD V-12

1919

Few automobile manufacturers have enjoyed the success Packard was having in 1919. As a matter-of-fact, Packard had been riding the crest of a wave since 1917. A wave of their own making.

Packard had produced two racing cars, one dubbed "299" the other "905". The numerals came from the cubic inch displacement of the respective car's V-12 engines.

The "299" was a track car, with which, during a two year stint, Ralph DePalma won nearly every major prize in America. On a brutally cold November 16, 1917, at the Sheepshead Bay board track, DePalma drove "299" to a world's record of 616 miles in six hours. His average speed was a sensational 102.8 mph. Officials claimed it would have been as high as 110, if a thrown tire tread near the end of the run hadn't slowed his pace.

The enormous "905" was the direct forerunner to the Liberty aircraft engine. On July 28, 1917, over the same Sheepshead Bay course, Willard Rader blazed through a mile at 125.1 mph. He also clocked five miles at 124.5, and ten miles at 123.7. At Daytona Beach, on February 18, 1929, DePalma and the "905" thundered through the measured mile at 149.73 mph. to backup this claim to the land speed record, Ralph turned 92.71 for the standing start mile mark. The latter figure stood for thirty years.

Packard's romance with the V-12 was a two-edge attack on automotive engineering. Both the 299 and 905 had been spin-offs of their highly successful "Twin Six" passenger car engine.

After such performances on the track, the Indianapolis Motor Speedway honored Packard's achievements by naming the marque as pace car for 1919.

The car supplied to the speedway was, up to that time, the most advanced passenger car to serve as pacemaker. The Model 335 "Twin Six" was powered by a 60 degree V-12 engine with a 3 x 5 bore and stroke displacing a huge 424 cubic inches. This engine pumped out 90 smooth ponies at 3000 rpm. The car was so smooth, it could go from a standing start, to over 70 mph, in top gear, without a shift or shudder. The light weight crankshaft spun in three main bearings, carrying the load from twelve super-light aluminum pistons. This in a day when even a progressive company like Rolls-Royce still used steel slugs. Topside, the L-head's valves were run by a separate cam for each bank of cylinders. The complete engine weighed 400 pounds less then the 6-cylinder it was designed to replace.

No mention of the "Twin Six" can be made without a word concerning its designer, Jesse G. Vincent.

As unbelievable as it may seem, Mr. Vincent learned engineering though a mail order correspondence course! As if that wasn't enough, his education did not extend beyond the eighth grade! It was said, Vincent, like Fred Duesenberg, could glance at an experimental design and know instantly whether or not it would be successful. Vincent's career at Packard spanned forty years. Today, he is revered as one of the most influential men in automotive history.

Jesse G. Vincent proudly served as pace car driver.

Mr. Vincent's brother, Charles, was responsible for the preparation of the "299" and "905" racers.

In the 1919 500-mile classic, DePalma and "Ol' 299" looked like sure winners, until a wheel bearing failure caused a prolonged pit stop. The cream-colored beast still finished a more than creditable sixth.

1919

1919 Packard designer J.G. Vincent is already aboard the V-12 pacemaker ready for the pace lap. Car No. 4 is DePalma's factory entered Packard racer, while No. 3 is eventual winner Howdy Wilcox.

MARMON "34"

1920

Not since 1911, when Ray Harroun's fabled "Wasp" won the inaugural Indianapolis 500, had a Marmon seen more fanfare than our Model "34".

Located in Indianapolis, the firm of Nordyke and Marmon has always built a large, prestigious, dependable, luxury automobile. The "34" actually took shape in 1916, under the engineering genius of Howard Marmon, with assistance from Fred Moskovics and Alanson Brush. It was so durable and outstanding that, except for minor changes, it continued in much the same guise through 1924.

The power plant of our 1920 pacemaker has often been mistakenly listed as a V-16. While this is not surprising, given Marmon's great aptitude at designing many varied engine and components parts, the famous V-16 came much later.

The actual pacemaker was powered by a 6-cylinder 339.7 cubic inch engine developing 80 horsepower at 2450 rpm. Extensive use of aluminum was a Marmon trademark. The crankcase, cylinder head covers, timing gear case and cover were all aluminum. The ring carrying upper half of the pistons were aluminum, while the lower skirt was iron. Oil was ducted through a recess between these two halves, to pin bushings and rod bearings. Marmon's high pressure oiling system was improved, lubricating the entire valve-train through a hollow rocker arm pivot. This was the first automotive engine to discard the old shim-type main bearings in favor of the modern precision insert-type. A spherical cast-iron cylinder head was a new item. This engine was designated the 34B.

During wartime production of the Liberty and Hall-Scott engines, Marmon had achieved incredible manufacturing techniques. Machining tolerances as minute as .00025-inch had been exacted. All this progress and ability was put to use after World War I, and reflected on the great workmanship displayed in the 34B.

Marmon pioneered aluminum body and component parts, holding the weight of the 136-inch wheelbase car to only 3295 pounds. This particular Marmon sported an entirely aluminum body, produced by the Hume Body Company of Rochester, New York. The design is believed to be the work of W.E. Pierce. The radiator and frontal area was actually narrower than the standard Marmon. The design came to be known as the "Wasp Speedster."

Former champion racer, Barney Oldfield, was the pace car driver.

The "Wasp" was equipped with a special 3.0 to 1 rear axle ratio, and Barney led the field over the starting line at a then sensational 80 mph clip!

Even Barney's legendary rival Ralph DePalma—who was on the pole that year—remarked that Oldfield may have had the fastest car on the track.

Barney was so impressed with the Marmon, he acquired the car for his own use. He made eight coast to coast trips with it, promoting his new Oldfield Tire.

The car was so popular with the public, that Marmon announced production of the "Wasp Speedster" in August 1920. Marmon Racing Yellow, trimmed in black, with red wheel hub centers, were standard colors the following year. The speedy machine also sported a 0-100 speedometer.

While it's difficult to say for sure, this may be the first incident of a true Indy Pace Car replica being offered to the public—at least in any siginificant numbers.

1920

INDIANAPOLIS MOTOR SPEEDWAY

1920 Barney Oldfield in the Marmon Model '34.

H.C.S. "6"

1921

1921

After departing his namesake company in 1919, Harry C. Stutz didn't waste any time getting back into the automobile industry.

By 1920, Stutz was already building a car manufactured just up the street from his original factory. The "new Stutz" was called the HCS after Harry's own initials. The first year's production of nearly 800 cars at $2,900 each, looked like a promising beginning. The following year, however, America slipped into an economic recession. Sales of HCS Motor Company products dropped sharply.

It was hoped the announcement of HCS as the pacemaker for the 1921 Indianapolis 500, would help boost the company's lagging sales. Certainly Harry was thrilled, remembering how such an honor had helped his fledgling company in 1912. With renewed hope, Stutz named himself as pace car driver.

Our HCS Series 6 roadster was powered by a 6-cylinder Weidely engine displacing 288.6 cubic inches. The chassis had a wheelbase of 126-inches. Most everything on the HCS came from the hand and mind of Harry Stutz. High quality workmanship is evident on the few examples of the HCS extant today.

Harry had aimed at the average motorist in the street. The production cost of the HCS, however, precluded the marque being an economical means of transportation.

Even Tommy Milton's victory in the 1923 Indianapolis 500, at the wheel of a Miller powered car sponsored by HCS, failed to rejuvinate the slumping sales figures.

HCS production ended in 1925, and Harry divested himself of all interest in the company the following year.

Stutz had gone into the manufacture of fire trucks in 1919, but his success was little better than it had been with HCS. The Stutz Fire Engine Company failed in 1927. After going into receivership, this company was reorganized at Hartford City, Indiana, in 1931, as The New Stutz Fire Engine Company. A division of this company continued production until just prior to World War II.

In 1930, following a sensational divorce action, Harry moved to Orlando, Florida. Aligning himself with the famous Bellanca Airplane Company, Stutz designed a promising 4-cylinder aircraft engine.

Harry returned to Indianapolis, hoping to find backers for his new venture. Taken ill before the business trip, Harry's appendix ruptured just as he arrived at Indianapolis. He died June 26, 1930.

Today, Harry Stutz is usually remembered for the Stutz Bearcat. However—a monument of sorts—his gleaming brick and marble Stutz factory, still stands near downtown Indianapolis. The carved initial "S" can still be seen in the outer pillar tops.

Seated in the HCS Pacemaker, Harry Stutz surveys the racer behind him. The HCS was the first pace car to carry "Official Pace Car" lettering.

NATIONAL

The National Motor Car Company was often involved in successful auto racing enterprises. And why not? Arthur C. Newby, National's director was one of the founders of the Indianapolis Motor Speedway. Renowned racer Johnny Aitken, was one of the firm's chief engineers. Test driver, Joe Dawson, drove a National to victory in the 1912 500-mile race.

Newby and Aitken had long since departed the company when the 1922 Nationals hit the street.

This particular pacemaker is often erroneously referred to as an 8-cylinder. This would seem impossible, since there is no record of National ever producing an eight. The company went from a 12-cylinder in 1919, to a 6-cylinder in '22.

Apparently, our pacemaker was powered by a 6-cylinder 301.3 cubic inch overhead valve engine developing 71 horsepower. This was a very advanced engine, and proved to be very reliable. It could haul the 130-inch wheelbase "Sextet" along at a healthy 90 mph.

Cigar chomping Barney Oldfield was back for his second stint as pace car driver.

The recession of the early 1920s put National on the rocks. A merger with the Dixie Flyer and Jackson Companies, in '22, only prolonged National's existance another two years. The banks refused director Clarence A. Earl's request for an extension on major loans, and another Indianapolis based automotive company slipped into memory.

1922

1922

INDIANAPOLIS MOTOR SPEEDWAY

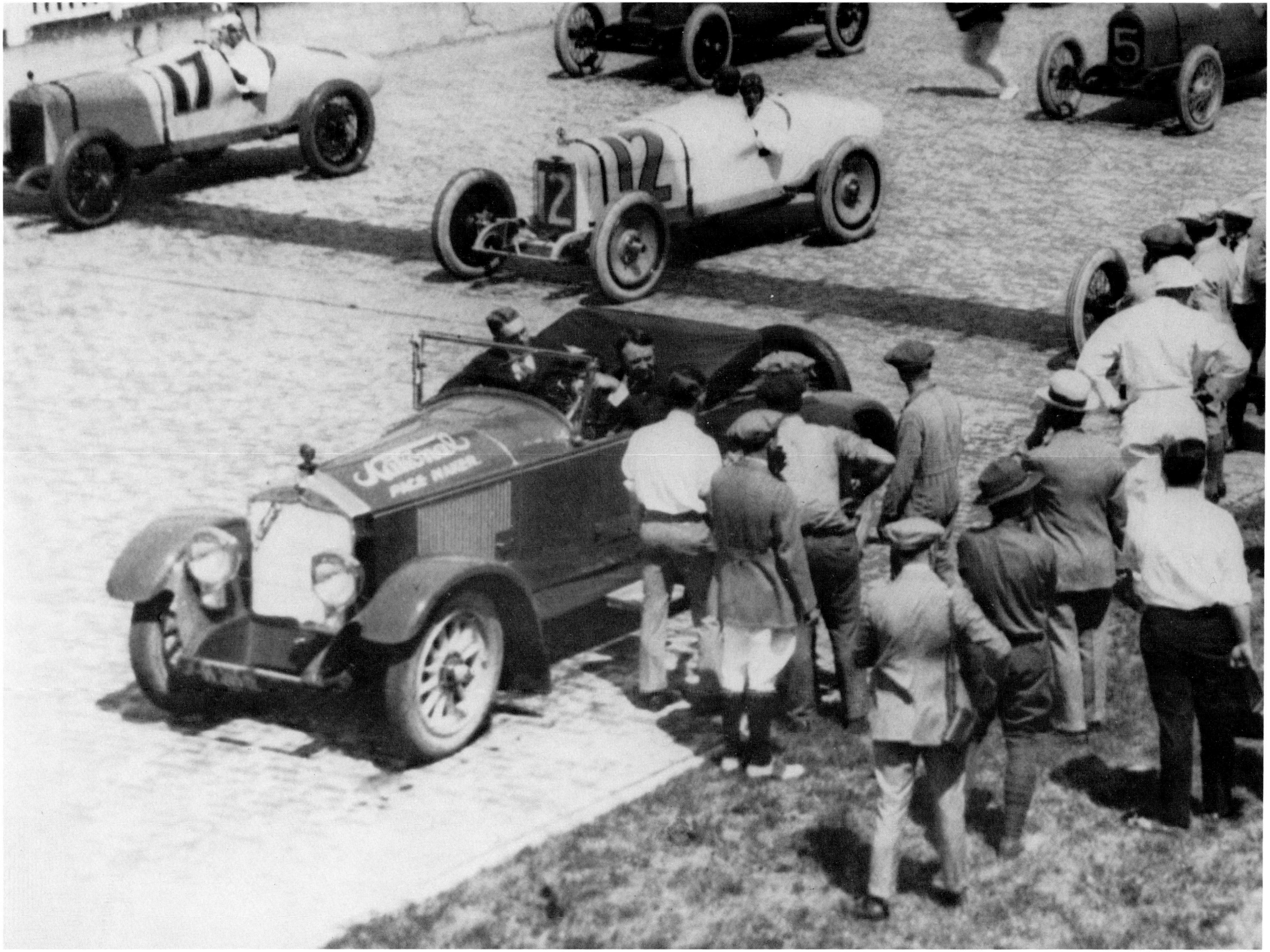

1922 National with Barney Oldfriend driving.

DUESENBERG

1923

If you're old enough to remember the Duesenberg era, you may recall their newspaper and magazine advertisements. A man seated in a lofty, paneled, baronial hall, listening to an enormous organ being played; a gentleman at the helm of a wind-swept racing yacht; a beautiful woman supervising her gardner near a golf course size lawn. They were simple line drawings, with a subtle statement: "He or She (as was the case) Drives A Duesenberg." No car appeared in the advertisements. No long statement of how great, wonderful, fast—the name Duesenberg said it all. The word lavish paled next to the name.

Handcrafted in a modest factory, employing less than fifty people, at the corner of Harding and Washington Streets, on Indianapolis' west side, the "Duesie" commanded the highest price of any American marque. Even the beautiful Cadillacs, Packards and Marmons of the day were a notch below the Duesenbergs. Indeed with the exception of Rolls-Royce or Bugatti, one seldom hears anything mentioned in the same breath with the thundering "Hoosier Limousines."

In April 1923, an "A" Series Duesenberg touring car orbited the Indianapolis Motor Speedway on a simulated trans-continental run. The Duesie completed the non-stop 3155 mile fifty hour run averaging nearly 63 mph. Refueling, driver changes, even a spark plug replacement was completed at speed. In another instance, again at the speedway, another Duesenberg ran for three full weeks, covering over 18,000 miles.

After those two performances, choosing the Duesenberg as the 1923 pace car seemed a mere formality. It was the icing on the cake.

Although our "A" Series did not have the sensational lines of the later "J" or "SJ" Series, the workmanship was outstanding—unmistakably Duesenberg.

In reality, Fred and his brother August Duesenberg, had been producing passenger cars less than two years when the "A" was chosen pacemaker!

They had been in the aviation and racing engine business, and their powerful passenger car motor was a derivative of the latter.

Our pace car was powered by a straight-8 overhead-camshaft engine. It displaced 259.7 cubic inches producing 90 horsepower. The big 134-inch wheelbase car could attain 100 mph with ease. Four wheel hydraulic brakes were a pioneering standard feature.

Since Duesenberg contracted work to several different coach builders, and records are incomplete, exact identification is difficult. Our pacemaker appears to be the handy work of Millspaugh and Irish. In the style of the times, it carried twin side-mounted tires on either side of the cowling.

Fred Duesenberg was the proud driver of the pace car. After stopping on the pit apron, following the start, he reportedly said, "Felt like I should have taken another lap with 'em!"

Although there are no actual figures, it's safe to say there were as few as 500 "A" Series Duesies built between 1921 and '26. There are no accurate figures on the '23 model. The price tag of $6,500 custom-made car hurt the sales badly. One must realize a Buick, for example, could be purchased for about $1,500.

Today, most anything with four wheels, carrying the Duesenberg name, will fetch $300,000 at auction.

Racers completely designed by the Duesenbergs, powered by their straight-8 engine, won the Indianapolis 500 in 1924, '25 and '27.

While the Duesenberg brothers were the toast of America's automotive world, their genius did not extend into business and money management. Fred invented the hydraulic brake, but failed to take out a patent on it. It was said he gave engine designs away—one to his friend Harry Stutz.

1923

When E.L. Cord took over the financially ill company in '28, he brought with him what was considered in that day, sound business judgement. After the Wall Street disaster, however, the buyers for such cars dissapeared. The company survived on a car to car basis until '37.

Fred Duesenberg had died in July 1932.

The "Duesenberg Plant" as it was always known—no matter how many other businesses resided there—is no more. On the same grounds stands the new headquarters of the Metro Bus Company. It would seem the property is destined to continue in the transportation industry.

COLE

1924

1924

Today, few people recall the Cole Motor Car Company. Perhaps fewer still, recognize the name of company founder Joseph Jaret Cole. In the years directly after World War I, this, no doubt, seemed impossible.

J.J. Cole was an automotive luminary of the same school as Stutz, Bugatti and Ferrari. He ascribed to their same basic principle. That is, he believed that style for style's sake—without reliable mechanical function—was utterly useless.

In the early formative years of the Indianapolis based firm, Cole, like the afore mentioned automotive magnates, believed racing helped sell his product. "Wild Bill" Endicott drove Coles to various wins. He even drove one in the 1911 Indianapolis 500.

Cole advertised his handsome, durable machine as the "Standardized Car." "Always One Season Ahead," was another motto. In 1918, just as the war was winding down, Cole coined "There's a touch of tomorrow in all Cole does today."

Indeed Cole was looking toward tomorrow. While most were predicting gloom and doom, Cole accurately forcast an up-turn in automotive sales. William Durant made at least two efforts to buy Cole out, but the futuristic minded Hoosier refused.

Purchasing the Inter-State Motor Company of Indiana, and other smaller firms, J.J. prepared to build some 30,000 cars per year. Such a figure was completely unheard of in that era, but obviously demonstrated what Cole believed the automotive business would be—someday.

Cole also believed that experts build expertly. Major components for his cars were purchased from outside manufacturers. None of these suppliers, however, were actually in the business of building cars. He even contracted with General Motors' Northway division to provide him with an advanced V-8 engine, similar to the Cadillac. Cole's cars were "assembled," but they sure didn't look or run that way. Nothing was left to chance, and the well appointed interiors were done in the finest leather or broad cloth.

Cole designed his "Aero-Eight" in '18. The following year, 6,225 of the sleek machines were sold. Cole was second only to Cadillac in the sale of luxury cars. The pleasing lines of the "Aero" became so popular, the basic lines of the design were only slightly altered seven years later.

The panic of the early 1920s, however, took its toll on Cole's fortunes. This was another reason the cars were little changed over the years. High priced cars were just not selling. Cole cut his prices, but since only the highest quality materials had been out into the cars, there were limits as to how far he could go. Sales continued to plummet.

The handwriting was on the wall, when the Indianapolis Motor Speedway chose a bright yellow Cole Master Model Roadster as pacemaker for the 1924 race.

"The speedway, in my estimation, has made it possible through racing and testing for the automobile industry to produce a better automobile in less time than would have been possible without the track," Mr. Cole said, upon hearing the news.

Our Series 890 was powered by the splendid 90 degree L-head V-8, created by Cole chief engineer Charles Crawford. It displaced 346.4 cubic inches with a bore and stroke of 3¼ x 4¼. This highly advanced engine pumped out 80 horsepower at 2600 rpm. Compression was a slight 3.6 to 1. The crankshaft was fully counterbalanced, utilizing the early type fork and blade arrangement for the bottom end. A Delco starter and ignition system set the whole thing in motion.

As already stated, this engine resembled Cadillac's V-8 in appearance. The Cole, however, had its own separate parts and completely different internal dimensions. The Cole was over 30 cubic inches larger than its GM counterpart.

A cone clutch assembly coupled with a Northway three-speed transmission, sent power to the rear wheels. Cole had long since featured a rugged differential, sporting oil-tempered chrome-nickel steel gears.

The fine handling 127¼-inch wheelbase chassis rode the Firestone 7.30 Gum Dipped balloon tires. The very first pace car to be so equipped. Dual sidemount tires were also featured.

INDIANAPOLIS MOTOR SPEEDWAY

Our pace car driver was long-time, Cole test driver, Louis Pettijohn.

Although a few cars were built for the 1925 model year, Cole terminated operation in October 1924. Many believe he had already decided to stop production before his roadster paced Indy.

An honest, forthright man, J.J. Cole—unlike many in similar straits—paid off all company debts. He even managed to pay off the stockholders. Once again, his foresight allowed him to get out while his company was still solvent.

Unfortunately, only ten months after the demise of his car, Mr. Cole died of a minor infection. Had death not taken him, perhaps his name would have appeared on the board of another large business concern. For J.J. Cole was recognized as a genius of organization.

1924 Cole V-8: Group in background include the owners of Speedway Fisher, Newby, Wheeler and Allison.

RICKENBACKER 8

1925

1925

Like the late Enzo Ferrari, Captain Eddie Rickenbacker used the emblem of an ace fighter pilot from World War I as the insignia for his automobile. Unlike Ferrari's prancing horse, Rickenbacker's Hat in the Ring emblem was not given to him by admiring friends. It was his own squadron emblem, carried into battle by America's ace of aces. Unfortunately, unlike the Commendatore, Rickenbacker's car production would not survive to the present day.

In 1925, "Rick's" phaeton was chosen as the Indianapolis 500 pace car. It was absolutely perfect publicity timing. The Rickenbacker was already a popular marque, in great demand. By March, the factory was some 2,000 cars behind new orders received. The pace car exposure, plus record runs by Cannon Ball Baker, helped sell 9,214 cars in 1925.

Our phaeton pacemaker was powered by a straight-8 engine. The "Vertical 8" had a bore and stroke of 3¼ x 4¾ measuring out to 315 cubic inches producing 84 horsepower. The camshaft ran completely submerged in oil, encased in an oil-tight compartment, completely separate from the crankcase. It had dual ignition, and dual mufflers via a "split-manifold." The beefy crankshaft ran in nine main bearings, sporting a dual flywheel, one on either end of the shaft. This latter feature made the engine—according to the advertising—vibration proof. From all reports, this was true, and certainly made "Rick's car" a unique machine in that day. The wheelbase was 121.5-inches, giving a smooth ride.

Another feature was the Rickenbacker's powerful four wheel mechanical brakes. Rickenbacker owners liked to bet they could stop quicker than drivers of other makes.

The car was designed by E.R. Evans. Experimental engineering was carried out by Ray McNamara, a veteran driver of the Glidden Tours.

It had to be a thrill for Captain Eddie, leading the 25-car field over the starting line, in a car bearing his name. Many close associates said it was the proudest day of his life.

In Greek mythology, Phaethon drove a sun-chariot across the sky, lost control, and was struck down by a thunderbolt. So it was with our phaeton—all other Rickenbacker models.

Only two short years after pacing the 500, the Rickenbacker went out of production. Rising costs, and a collapse of the dealer network, were the main causes.

In the five years the marque was built, there were approximately 34,500 Rickenbacker cars produced.

Until 1932, the Rickenbacker engine designs were used in the German Audi.

By 1928, Captain Eddie had other interests. He was the new owner of the Indianapolis Motor Speedway.

Captain Eddie Rickenbacker with group of Speedway officials in 1925.

CHRYSLER IMPERIAL

1926

Walter P. Chrysler claimed he fought his way to, from, and through school. A native of Kansas, Chrysler came from humble beginnings. He never lost contact with the common man.

In 1919, after attaining the position of vice president of General Motors, Chrysler abruptly left the firm following a disagreement with William C. Durant. Five years later, Chrysler acquired the faltering Maxwell Motor Car Company.

By 1926, Chrysler's neat, dependable, affordable cars had drawn the attention of the Indianapols Motor Speedway. The Chrysler Imperial was honored as the pace car, and the added public exposure did nothing but help. Company sales went from twenty-seventh to fifth place. In that year, some 129,565 Chryslers were sold.

Since our pacemaking roadster could attain 80 mph, it was designated the Model "80". In that day, 80 mph was a very high speed for the open road. It wasn't often a car priced below Cadillac, Lincoln and Pierce-Arrow was capable of such performance.

The Imperial was powered by a 6-cylinder engine of 288.7 cubic inches developing 92 horsepower at 3000 rpm. The pistons were made of Lynite aluminum alloy. The engine was designed by J.B. Macauley, Chrysler's chief of dynamometer testing. A standard three-speed transmission with chrome-steel gears and a roller-bearing output shaft, transferred power to a 4.60 to 1 gear ratio differential.

Our pace car driver was the legendary Louis Chevrolet, who reportedly fell in love with the "quick" roadster.

In June 1926, Floyd Clymer drove a stock Imperial from Denver to Kansas City, in 13 hours 56 minutes, averaging 51.8 mph. This was a passenger car record speed for any distance over 500 miles. It's all the more remarkable, when one learns only 200 of the 702 miles covered were paved!

1926

1926 Chrysler Imperial "80" Louis Cheverolet is driver.

LA SALLE

1927

1927

Introduced by General Motors in 1927, as a sporty running mate to the Cadillac, the La Salle soon became known as the "little Cadillac" or the Cadillac's "little brother."

Designed by the "father of automobile designers," the great Harley Earl, at the request of Cadillac's president, Lawrence P. Fisher, La Salle offered a truly fine car at a considerable savings of some $1130 compared to the Cadillac. The popularity of its sales, brought La Salle to the attention of Indianapolis Motor Speedway officials, who selected the new car as pacemaker for 1927.

The pace car was a Series 303 roadster, deriving its name from the 303 cubic inch L-head V-8 engine under its stylish hood. This smooth running power plant, with a bore and stroke of 3-1/8 x 4-15/16, produced 75 horsepower at 3000 rpm. The crankshaft ran in three main bearings. Mechanical valve lifters with rollers riding directly on the camshaft operated the valves. The carburetor was a C.F. Johnson model, manufactured by Cadillac. This rather exotic engine was the La Salle's main link to Cadillac.

Actually, the La Salle power plant was quite different, at least internally, from previous Cadillac V-8s. It had modern side by side connecting rods instead of the earlier fork-and-blade layout. Most of the engine work was done under the guidance of Ernest W. Seaholm and W.R. Strickland, engineers of the fabulous V-16 and V-12 Cadillac engines. Much of their work has carried directly over into modern engines of today. In this area, our pace car was helping push back the horizons of internal combustion engineering.

The 125-inch wheelbase chassis was rather long for a lower priced roadster. This undoubtedly helped with the ride, and gave it a certain "Cadillac look."

Willard "Big Boy" Rader, also known as Bill, made his debut as pace car driver.

Rader was a famous long distance test driver of the era. In June 1927, "Big Boy" and other drivers, participated in a testing session at The General Motors Proving Grounds, located at Milford, Michigan. In the test, a La Salle covered 951.87 miles averaging 95.3 mph for nearly ten hours. A tremendous achievement for a newly designed automobile, especially when one realizes that George Souders' winning Duesenberg averaged only 97.545 mph in winning the 500 that year.

1927 La Salle V-8 awaits the start of the race.

MARMON "78"

1928

By 1928, Marmon, under the direction of George M. Williams, was riding a new crest of popularity. By then, the firm was called the Marmon Motor Car Company. They even sponsored two of Earl Cooper's Miller powered race cars in the 500. Johnny Seymour and Pete Kreis were the drivers. Both machines failed to finish.

The beautiful Marmon Model "78" was selected as pacemaker for the 1928 Indianapolis 500.

A straight-8 overhead valve engine displacing 216.8 cubic inches, cranking out 86 horsepower at 3400 rpm, powered our roadster.

Joe Dawson, who drove a National to victory in the 1912 Indianapolis 500, served as pace car driver. Dawson was the first former Indy winner to pace the starting field. Joe was also a testdriver for Marmon. He is often credited with helping Marmon's products become the durable machines they were.

This engine, however, was not the work of Howard Marmon. The straight-8 was the design of engineer Barney Roos.

Disillusioned with designs he considered boring and ordinary, Mr. Marmon had established a separate design office. Here, he designed the famous V-16 engine that saw production in 1931.

Marmon sales plummeted during the depression, and production ended in 1933. The following year, Harry Miller and Preston Tucker made an attempt to revive the marque. This effort failed, and the company funds were liquidated in 1937.

Howard's brother, Walter C. Marmon, and Col. Arthur W. Harrington, formed the Marmon Harrington Company in 1931. Until closing its doors in July 1963, the operation produced trucks, busses and trollies. Ironically, they were located in the former Duesenberg plant.

As a side light to this story: A number of years after Marmon's demise, a man the author's father knew—a former Marmon employee—wanted to sell a brand new Marmon roadster. Upon close inspection, the vehicle had traits of several different Marmon designs. It transpired that, over a period of ten years, the employee had built his own Marmon "special." His method was somewhat like singer Johnny Cash's song "One Piece At A Time."

It's doubtful if he ever sold it!

1928

INDIANAPOLIS MOTOR SPEEDWAY

1928 Marmon Model 78 with Joe Dawson, the 1912 winner, as the driver.

STUDEBAKER

1929

1929

If you live in the United States, it's quite possible your ancestors migrated across the country in a Studebaker covered wagon.

In 1852, brothers Henry and Clem Studebaker started business in South Bend, Indiana. The marque was already a top name in the automotive world, when the Indianapolis Motor Speedway held its first 500-mile race in 1911.

In 1929, Studebaker, on the basis of speed and endurance records unmatched by any other make car of that day, was honored as pacemaker. The firm supplied the speedway with a handsome Model F10 President roadster.

Our pacemaker was powered by an L-head straight-8 engine displacing 337 cubic inches with a bore and stroke of 3-1/2 x 4-3/8. This combination produced 114 horsepower at 3200 rpm. The crankshaft turned in five main bearings. The Stromberg carburetor, sporting an automatic choke, was mounted on an improved intake manifold. Studebaker took pride in calling itself, "the world's predominant manufacturer of 8-cylinder engines."

The new double drop frame and semi-floating rear axle, gave the 125-inch wheelbase machine a firm, but comfortable ride.

A good deal of chrome, including Budd wire wheels, was evident on the President. The stylish roadster carried the message "500 Mile Race Pace Maker" on its fold down top. In publicity releases, it was often photographed with Mae West at the wheel.

George Hunt was the pace car driver.

1929 Studebaker President, George Hunt was the driver.

CORD L-29

1930

By 1930, after helping establish Duesenberg as a world renowned marque, E.L. Cord was well on his way to establishing another great American car.

Cord believed Harry Stutz had been correct concerning the public's desire for a sports car such as the Bearcat. He deviated from the Bearcat idea, however, believing Americans wanted a larger, more stylish car.

Cord spared no expense on his new front-wheel-drive creation. He hired only the best engineers and body builders to fabricate a fast, dependable, sporty machine. His efforts did not go unrewarded.

The Cord L-29 cabriolet, designed by Alan Leamy, was soon the talk of the automotive world. Leamy's rakish, clean design was long, low, and seemed to be in motion even when standing still. It quickly drew the attention of Indianapolis Motor Speedway officials, and was perhaps the most elegant pace car of the 1930s. In this decade of dignified, luxury pacemakers, which included such names as Cadillac, Lincoln, Chrysler, and Packard, this statement alone, says much about the L-29.

Development of the L-29 took place at the Duesenberg plant in Indianapolis. Later, some of the engineering duties were shifted to the Auburn factory, Auburn, Indiana.

The beautiful creation was powered by a Lycoming straight-8 L-head engine of 298.6 cubic inches with a bore and stroke of 3¼ x 4½. The crankshaft was counterbalanced, running in five main bearings. A twin-throat Schebler updraft carburetor, receiving gasoline via a mechanical pump, controlled fuel flow. The engine was rated at 125 horsepower when turning 3600 rpm. Compression was 5.25 to 1, and the valve lifters were the solid type.

The clutch was a single dry plate of 11 inches diameter, designed by the Long Manufacturing Company. Power went through a Detroit 3-speed selective transmission, on its way to a Columbia inverted hypoid differential.

The union of the differential and the front-wheel-drive unit were engineered by the great C.W. Van Ranst. "Van" had been the chief engineer and guiding hand behind many of the Chevrolet brothers successes at Indianapolis.

Brakes were internal four-wheel hydraulic, running in pressed steel drums of 12 and 15 inch diameter, front and rear, respectively.

Front suspension consisted of 22 inch double quarter-elliptic springs, while the rear were 62 inch semi-elliptic riding on an I-beam axle. The ride was controlled by Houdaille adjustable hydraulic shock absorbers. Although the actual pace car wheelbase is unknown, the standard measurement was 137.5-inches. This appears to be a likely figure for our cabriolet.

The wire wheels had knock-off hubs and carried 7.00 x 18 whitewall tires. This included the twin-sidemounted wheels, outside rearview mirrors, dual sychromous horns, and courtesy lights on the running boards were other features. It appears our pacemaker was equipped with automatic radiator shutters, to contol engine heat.

The Gemmer work and roller steering made a surprisingly easy handling car, especially in view of the heavy front-wheel-drive unit. The steering wheel traveled 3⅓ turns from lock to lock.

The gear shift lever passed through a fully instrumented dashboard, that included gasoline and oil level gauges, engine thermometer, oil pressure and amp gauges.

Race driver Wade Morton was assigned as pace car driver. Certainly, he was photographed in the car during the month of May. Legend, however, says that E.L. Cord, himself, drove the pace lap. Skip Marketti, Executive Director of the Auburn-Cord-Duesenberg Museum, has also voiced this opinion.

Whatever the case, it was a beautifully turned-out machine. One of the great classic one-time-only pacemakers at Indy.

In August 1937, only seven years after pacing the 500, Cord, like Duesenberg and Marmon went onto the financial rocks. Cord lost control of his company and it was all over.

On January 2, 1974, Errett Lobban Cord died in relative obscurity in Reno, Nevada.

1930

1930 Cord with E.L. Cord.

1930 Cord with driver E.L. Cord and Eddie Eddenburn.

E.L. Cord and the 1930 Pace Car.

CADILLAC

1931

In 1931, Cadillac produced a completely new car. The Model "370" was so sporty and sharp looking, the Indianapolis Motor Speedway decided to name it as pace car.

The numeral came from the engine displacement of 370 cubic inches. Our pacemaking roadster could loaf along at an easy cruising speed of 70 mph, and 85 was a cinch. The reason was the revolutionary new engine—the Cadillac V-12. Although other manufacturers had build V-12s—Cadillac even had a V-16—this was a first for the line. The engine produced 135 horsepower at 3400 rpm. It was a very quick car off the line, and "Caddy" owners reveled in one of the fastest accelerating cars around. One reason for this, was improved breathing through overhead valves. An arrangement not so common in passenger cars of that era. The valves were actuated by pushrods and rocker arms much like those of later V-8 engines.

This power plant was designed by the same gentlemen—Ernest W. Seaholm and W.R. Strickland—who gave us the advanced V-8 engine in the '27 La Salle. Basically they cut four cylinders off the existing V-16 engine to produce the V-12. The painstaking work of Seaholm, however, made this engine a smooth piece of work all its own. What Jesse Vincent had been to Packard, Seaholm was to the Cadillac Division of General Motors.

Our pace car's beautiful body lines were the work of the Fleetwood Body Company. The distinctive hood sported five vent doors on either side, giving the "370" a racey appearance. Something quite unique for a luxury car of that era.

Our pace car driver was Willard "Big Boy" Rader, back to lead the field for a second time.

In another time, the "370" roadster would have produced tremendous sales. Americans, mired deep in the depression, couldn't afford the basic price of $3795.

Nevertheless, it made a beautiful pace car.

1931

1931 Cadillac - Driver: unknown; passenger: T.E. "Pop" Myers, Supt./Grounds-GM, Indianapolis Motor Speedway.

LINCOLN

1932

Without a doubt, the Indianapolis Motor Speedway choice for pacemaker in 1932, was one of the sharpest cars of the depression riddled decade. Namely, the Model KB Lincoln roadster.

The guy who wrote the pop song "Hot Rod Lincoln" may not have had the KB in mind, but Edsel Ford certainly wanted it to be a high performance car. After the Ford Motor Company purchased Lincoln from the Leland family in '22, Edsel made the marque his pet project. He transformed the staid, but bland Lincoln into a fresh, stylish motoring experience. It especially pleased him to send a KB to Indianapolis, as pace car.

It was a proud moment in Ford history. His father Henry, and two sons, Henry II, and Benson Ford accompanied Edsel to Indianapolis.

Our sleek KB was a Murphy Sports Roadster, powered by a V-12 engine. This L-head motor was similar to the Packard and Cadillac multi-cylinder units. Its bore and stroke was 3¼ x 4½ displacing 448 cubic inches and developed 150 horsepower at 3400 rpm. The cylinder banks stood at a 65 degree angle. A polished and balanced crankshaft 39¼ inches long, weighing ninety-three pounds, was cranked over by carefully balanced rods and matched aluminum pistons. The huge main bearing supported nearly ⅓ of the crankshaft length. The old fork and blade connecting rod technique was a hold over from Leland. The drop-forged camshaft incorporated an automatic chain tensioner, removing slack from the timing gear. Frank Johnson—Edsel Ford's right hand man at Lincoln—was chief engineer of this impressive power plant. He was assisted by Jack Wharam and Fred Wellborn.

Anyone around in those days, will tell you the 150 horse rating was conservative, to say the least. In a special road test, only one new car in the entire world—an Alfa Romeo sports car—could out accelerate the V-12 KB. Our roadster would easily top 95 mph.

The 145-inch wheelbase chassis was amazingly rigid. Power was transferred through a three-speed, free-wheeling transmission via a torque-tube to a floating rear axle. Since Henry Ford distrusted hydraulic brakes, the Lincoln was fitted with vacuum-assisted mechanical Bendix units.

Who better to serve as pace car driver than the man responsible for this striking automobile—Edsel Ford.

1932

INDIANAPOLIS MOTOR SPEEDWAY

1932 Lincoln and Pace Car driver Edsel Ford.

CHRYSLER IMPERIAL

1933

The beautiful Imperial Custom Eight convertible, was our pacemaker in 1933.

This wonderfully turned out roadster, the last one Chrysler would produce, was powered by a straight-8 L-head engine. This motor was produced in several different displacements and compression combinations. From all indications, our Imperial was spared nothing. The engine displaced 384.8 cubic inches with a bore and stroke of 3½ x 5 producing 135 horses at 3200 rpm. The long crankshaft had nine main bearings for support. A downdraft Stromberg carburetor fed gasoline to the 5.8 to 1 compression head and pistons. The new improved steel alloy exhaust valves and seats, were put through their paces by solid valve lifters, urged on by a single in block camshaft. Delco Remy ignition made the spark.

A new three-speed silent helical gear transmission received power through a vacuum assisted clutch. Lockheed hydraulic brakes brought the heavy 4,910 pound machine to a safe stop.

Our 146-inch wheelbase pacer carried a semi-custom body by LeBaron. Only nine of these were built, featuring lower ground clearance, six chrome metal spoke wheels, (two were sidemounts) chrome ventilator hood doors and twin external trumpet horns positioned on either side of the sloping V-grille.

Pace car driver, Byron Foy, probably didn't realize he would pace the largest field—42 cars—in Indianapolis 500 history.

The Golden Seal Special, powered by a Chrysler straight-8 engine, was driven to fourteenth place by Raoul Riganti. This car also made use of Chrsyler axles, fore and aft, as well as the new helical gear transmission.

1933

Byron Foy in the 1933 Chrysler Imperial Phaeton.

LA SALLE

1934

By 1934, the La Salle had outgrown the stigma of the so-called "little brother" of the Cadillac. Gone were the shared features of the "Caddy," including the V-8 engine.

In truth, General Motors planned on dropping the La Salle after '33. Designer Harley Earl had other ideas. It was Earl's new body styling that saved the line from a premature demise.

When the Indianapolis Motor Speedway chose a little machine as pace car in '34, the La Salle Series 350 was a car all its own, with its own identity.

The identity problem had been a stumbling block for the marque since its inception. Sales had steadily fallen since 1930. The redesigning, plus the speedway limelight, helped revive the sales trend.

Our roadster was powered by an L-head straight-8 of 240.3 cubic inches with a bore and stroke of 3 x 4¼. This highly advanced engine produced 95 horsepower at 3700 rpm. The cast iron cylinder block and crankcase were poured as an integral unit. Aluminum pistons, a five main bearing crankshaft and a Stromberg Duplex down-draft carburetor with automatic choke, were added features. The compression ratio was 6.5 to 1, and the valves were actuated by mechanical lifters.

Actually, despite all claims to the contrary, this engine was very much like the Oldsmobile, and was probably assembled in the Cadillac plant.

A single plate clutch and selective synchro transmission, sent torque to a Hotchkiss semi-floating rear axle with 4.78 to 1 spiral bevel gearing.

The La Salle offered a $650 reduction in its basic price. Even though it sold for only $1595, the La Salle had hydraulic brakes as a standard feature.

The new body, by Fleetwood, was a graceful, streamlined creation for its day. The tall, narrow grille became a trademark, as did the five bubble-shaped vents on either side of the hood. The bullet-shaped headlights attached to the hood, and chrome trim on the long pontoon fenders, made the La Salle's styling appear ten years ahead of its time. The double-bar bumpers were hung on telescoping spring mounts. The windshield was a modern one-piece style.

"Knee-Action" independent front suspension was a new feature, giving the 119-inch wheelbase car a better ride than much larger cars with beam axles. The comfortable ride, alone, was a huge selling point, making the La Salle one of the more popular cars of 1934.

Back for his third term as pace car driver, was Willard Rader.

1934

Eddie Rickenbacker and others with the 1934 LaSalle Pace Car.

1934 LaSalle in action at the start of the 500.

1934 LaSalle with driver "Big Boy" Raeder and Captain Eddie Rickenbacker, owner of the Indianapolis Motor Speedway.

FORD

1935

For many years, Ford has been the trendsetter in the lower priced automobile market. The year 1935, was to see a big influx of America's most popular car, at Indianapolis.

In that year, the Ford Motor Company commissioned Harry Miller to build a fleet of ten front-wheel-drive race cars. Miller's design centered around the tough Ford flathead V-8 engine. Only four of them made the race. The ill-placed steering gear failed on all four, long before the 500 miles were completed.

Our pacemaker, however, suffered no such problems, as Ford went on to be the largest selling car in America, during '35.

The Ford Model 48 convertible sedan, with its rakish good looks, was powered by the familiar 90 degree L-head cast iron V-8 dispacing 221 cubic inches with a bore and stroke of 3-1/16 x 3-3/4 cranking out 85 horsepower at 3800 rpm. The crankshaft ran in three main bearings. It had an improved camshaft and mechanical valve lifters. A better crankcase ventilation system helped control oil foaming. In June '35, Ford produced their two-millionth V-8 engine. The little cast iron wonder would be the mainstay of hot rodders for years to come.

The 112-inch wheelbase frame and rear axle were beefed up, but the archaic suspension system of a single transverse leaf spring, fore and aft, still held sway—if you'll pardon the phrase—at Ford. Old Henry was still clinging to mechanical brakes, as well as wire wheels.

The narrower radiator grille had less V-shape, and the side hood louvers were accentuated with three bright chrome strips. New headlights and twin taillights were an added feature. The overall shape was rounder and lower.

The pace car driver for this neat little machine was Dearborn Branch exective, Harry Mack.

1935

INDIANAPOLIS MOTOR SPEEDWAY

Amelia Earhart in the 1935 Ford.

PACKARD

1936

Even though the Packard 120 was far from a cheap mode of transportation, it was, at a base price of $980, the lowest priced of the line in 1936. Between August 1935 and August '36, nearly 51,000 of the striking 120s were sold, The clean efficient styling of this member of Packard's Fourteenth Series, had much to do with the sales. Advance publicity of the car had orders streaming from Packard showrooms to the factory.

Our convertible sedan was powered by a straight-8 L-head engine displacing 282 cubic inches with a bore and stroke of 3¼ x 4¼ producing 120 horsepower. This engine was so powerful and durable, that it continued to be used, unchanged, through the 1947 Packard Clippers.

Many buyers thought the 120 acquired its name from the horsepower rating. In reality, it came from the 120-inch wheelbase chassis. The Saf-T-Flex independent front suspension gave the sporty vehicle a great ride. It was not until after World War II, that Rolls-Royce, Bentley and other such marques of renown, went to independent suspension.

After the 120 had been chosen as pace car, Packard president Alvan Macauley asked former two-time Indianapols winner, Tommy Milton, if he'd drive the pacemaker. At that time, Milton was a chief development engineer at Packard. Very pleased, Tommy accepted on one condition. "I'd like to have your assurance that the pacemaker will be given to the winner," Milton offered, "in recognition of the honor of being invited." Mr. Macauley agreed, and a precedent was set that continues to the present.

After the grueling 1936 race, Milton presented the keys to the Packard 120 to a smiling Louie Meyer. The first three-time Indianapolis 500 winner, and the first to receive a pace car as one of the accessory prizes.

Packard fell on hard times during the 1950s. Their purchase of Studebaker, in '54, failed to halt their slide. The venerable name disappeared from the automotive list in July 1958.

Packard had been a great influence in the auto industry. They were one, if not the first, to adopt the steering wheel as standard equipment, replacing the tiller. Packard also liked to get their models out before the competition. Doing their best to debut their new cars in August—September at the latest. A trend continued by every American auto maker to the present day.

1936

Tommy Milton, Winner of the 1921 and 1923 500's with the 1936 Packard 120 Pace Car.

Preston Tucker and L.G. Epsteen, 1936 Packard 120.

Louie Meyer, 1st to win pace car receives his 1936 award.

LA SALLE

1937

An upturn in sales prompted Cadillac to upscale the La Salle for 1937. Once again, it was powered by the Cadillac L-head V-8 displacing 322 cubic inches with a bore and stroke of 3-3/8 x 4-1/2. This engine, borrowed from the 1936 Cadillac Series 60, churned out 125 horsepower at 3400 rpm. As in the '27 model, the block and crankcase were integral. The crankshaft ran in three main bearings. Compression was either 6.25 to 1, or the optional 5.75 to 1. The valves were a good deal quieter than before, since they were operated by hydraulic lifters. This car was equipped with the famous two-float carburetor which prevented fuel starvation during sharp turns.

The now familiar independent suspension was enhanced even further by an addition of a torsional stabilizer on the front, to reduce oversteer, and a Panhard rod at the rear. The tires were 7.00 x 16, and as usual, on La Salle, were stopped by hydraulic brakes on all four wheels.

A synchro transmission sent the twist to a Hotchkiss semi-floating rear axle with 3.92 to 1 hypoid gearing.

Our Series 37-50 roadster pacemaker was back on the 125-inch wheelbase frame. The chassis was much stiffer, however, and some 2½ inches lower than previous models.

Always a trendsetter, the La Salle was neater, more streamlined in appearance, than ever before. New grille, headlights and more chrome made it an eye-catching automobile. The five bubble-shaped hood vents, had been replaced by seven louvered panels on either side of the hood. Replacing the one-piece windshield was a V-shaped two-piece style with a center post.

Our pace car driver was the great Ralph DePalma, winner of the 1915 Indianapolis 500-mile race. Ralph became the second former winner to serve in this capacity. The first had been Joe Dawson in 1928.

La Salle's record sales of 32,005 units in '37, prompted GM to retain the marque until 1940. Thereafter, the old problem of being "too much like a Cadillac" reared it head once more. The line was also in direct competition to Buick, and GM saw no reason for it to continue.

Every now and then, one hears of a revival of the name La Salle. In 1955, two GM showcars were called La Salle. Some early Buick Riviera and Corvair prototypes carried the name, but never saw production.

1937

INDIANAPOLIS MOTOR SPEEDWAY

Ralph DePalma (driver) and T.E. "Pop" Myers in the 1937 LaSalle Pacemaker.

DePalma and Pace Car pose before the '37 race.

Pace Lap 1937 with a '37 LaSalle leading the field.

HUDSON 112

1938

In 1909, when Ray Chapin, Howard Coffin, James Brady and Frederick Bezner built their first automobile, they had no name for their product. They decided to name it after their most illustrious inventor. Department store impresario J.L. Hudson give his permission, and the rest is history.

Hudson hit their zenith during the early 1930s, while still combined with Essex and the popular Essex Terraplane.

Always known for engineering, performance and value without much fanfare or fancy gadgets, Hudson got into the small economy car market in 1938.

In view of this new trend—at least for Hudson—Indianapolis Motor Speedway officials chose the "sized-down" Model 112 as the pace car. Cross country road tests of the 112, by such Indianapolis star drivers as Ted Horn, Babe Stapp, Chet Miller and Ira Vail also helped to gain the speedway and public attention.

Our 112 convertible's name was derived from its small wheelbase of only 112-inches. The engine was a small 6-cylinder of only 190.8 cubic inches. Power was low—only 86 horses at a blistering 4,000 rpm. In an era when 12 or 13 miles to the gallon was considered good, the little 112 could brag of 24 miles-per-gallon. There were drawbacks, however.

From a standing start, it took all of 35 seconds to reach 60 mph. The little machine could barely top 70 mph, causing some people to wonder if it could "escape" the charging starting field.

Our pace car driver, Stu Baits, wasn't worried, though. You see, he's designed the pacemaker from the ground up. Of course, his confidence was rewarded.

1938

INDIANAPOLIS MOTOR SPEEDWAY

Stuart Baits in the 1938 Hudson 112 Pacemaker.

BUICK

1939

Not many examples of this ambitious Roadmaster 80 Series four-door phaeton remain. The 1939 model saw Buick's first real attempts at streamlining and smaller frontal area. Chief Engineer Charles A. Chayne took his cue from many popular European marques of the time, in trying to free-up air-flow. The '39 model was constructed of thinner than normal body panels, lightening the load carried by the 133-inch wheelbase frame.

In theory, the chassis and suspension were completely new. Modern day coil springs were used on all four corners. Since there was no apparent need for rear anchor points for leaf springs, the frame was shortened. This saved additional weight, but weakened the rear of the car. The trunk area could not support a heavy load. A recall to extend the frame became necessary to correct this.

Our Roadmaster was the first model Buick to adopt turn signals as standard equipment. These were on the rear, only. The very first push-button radios came out on this model.

The 320.2 cubic inch overhead valve straight-8 with a bore and a stroke of 3-7/16 x 4-5/16 produced 141 horsepower at 3600 rpm. The crankshaft was a five main bearing unit. This engine was very efficient and quiet for a motor of that period. Many features of its valve train were incorporated into the Buick V-8 after World War II. Mechanical valve lifters operating long pushrods and rocker arms were put into action by a single camshaft located deep in the block. Compression was 6.35 to 1, drawing gasoline from a Stromberg carburetor.

Charlie Cayne drove the pace car himself, in Buick's first, but certainly not last, Indy appearance.

1939

INDIANAPOLIS MOTOR SPEEDWAY

BUICK ROADMASTER
OFFICIAL PACE CAR
500-MILE-RACE
INDIANAPOLIS
MAY-30-1939

STUDEBAKER

1940

With the advent of the stock block two-man cars of the depression era, Studebaker became a constant fixture at Indianapolis.

In the 1932 Indy 500, Cliff Bergere finished third, driving a Studebaker powered entry. His teammate, Zeke Meyer, brought another "Stude" home sixth.

The following year, Studebaker powered cars driven by Dave Evans, Tony Gulotta, Russ Snowberger, Zeke Meyer, Luther Johnson, Bergere and L.L. Corum filled out the sixth through twelfth finishing positions, respectively.

Each year, thereafter, until 1939, when the so-called "junk-yard formula" ended, at least one of the reliable straight-8 "South Benders" made the starting field.

In July 1939, two completely stock Studebaker Champion two-door sedans circled the Indianapolis Motor Speedway for 15,000 miles. Their speed of 62 mph, while averaging over 19 mile-per-gallon, was a sensation.

On the strength of these achievements, the marque was selected as pace car for the 1940 race.

In an obvious attempt to promote their economy line of car, Studebaker sent a two-door Champion coupe, the first closed pace car, to Indianapolis.

The "Champ" was powered by a cast iron L-head 6-cylinder of 164.3 cubic inches with a bore and stroke of 3 x 3-7/8. This reliable little engine produced 78 horsepower at 4000 rpm. Compression was 6.50 to 1, and the crankshaft ran in four main bearings. Valve lifters were solid.

No figures on the exact wheelbase are available for the actual pace car. The Champion came in 110, 116.5 and 112-inch models.

Endurance and land speed record star, Ab Jenkins, served as pace car driver.

1940

The downtown Speedway office is the background for this 1940 photo of the Studebaker Pace Car. "Pop" Myers and Wilbur Shaw, '37 and '39 winner. Shaw won the 1940 race, also.

CHRYSLER NEWPORT

1941

It has often been said: "A child once burned, fears fire a lifetime."

While Chrysler Corporation was hardly a child in the auto industry, they were still less than enthusiastic over passenger car streamlining. In truth, they were still smarting from their less than satisfactory results with the Airflow designs of the 1930s.

K.T. Keller, president of Chrysler, liked to keep his designers on their toes. He liked designs from outside the company to influence and stimulate their thinking.

By 1941, the LeBaron design concern had been purchased by Briggs Manufacturing Company. Their highly regarded designer, Alex Tremulis, thought it was time Chrysler shed the stigma of the despised Airflow. He set to work on a special streamlined creation called the Thunderbolt. Almost simultaneously, Ralph Roberts was put to work on a second project car—the Newport. Roberts was not a true designer, but he possessed an eye for prototype development.

Roberts' concept was a special machine, designed as a parade car. Only six of these long, low machines were ever produced.

If Keller had any doubts, they were quickly put to rest by the ooos and aaahs of car show patrons. Both the Thunderbolt and Newport drew great public attention. It was the Newport, however, that drew the attention of Indianapolis Motor Speedway officials. Their choice made the "NP" the only completely "special" non-production vehicle (Barney Oldfield would argue for his 1920 Marmon) to be a pace car.

Our dual cowl Newport phaeton was powered by an L-head straight-8 engine displacing 323.5 cubic inches. These cars have always been rated at 143 horsepower at 3400 rpm. Since this is 8 horsepower more than the stock engine of the same displacement, it may denote some added feature lost to us through the passing of time. The transmission was fluid drive.

The coachwork featured hidden headlights and a low road-hugging body. The front wheels had open fenderwells, but the rear were fully skirted. There were four cut away doors, with push-button door handles, making for easy access and style. There were no side windows, but our Newport sported two one-piece windshields. The retractable hard top was a forerunner of Ford's 1957 Skyliner. Hydraulically operated at the touch of a button, the roof disappeared into the back deck. This was a massive automobile, perhaps one of the heaviest to ever pace the Indy field. There were no joints or moldings between the body and fenders, however. The straight-through fenders gave the car an appearance of being stamped from a single piece of metal.

A 145.5-inch wheelbase Chrysler Imperial chassis, gave the Newport a surprisingly good ride.

The three-place bench seats, appointed in sumptuous leather, were sunk low in the cockpits. Deep carpeting covered the rest of the interior.

The Newport did much to reclaim Chrysler's styling image, and its influence could be seen in their post war designs.

A.B. Couture was the driver of our pace car.

This marvel of automobile art, owned for many years by Mr. Thomas Barrett III, currently resides in the Blackhawk Classic auto collection in California.

Since the Newport was a special show car, many people are under the impression Chrysler awarded the winners a regular production model. It appears, however, that no such award took place.

Apparently, neither Mauri Rose nor Floyd Davis, co-winners of the 1941 500-miler, received a pace car. "My dad told Floyd Davis to take the pace car," Mauri Rose, Jr. told the author. However, Floyd never received the car. "I don't believe any car was offered to either of them," Mrs. Floyd Davis recalled.

Whatever the case, it remains one of those strange quirks of Indy 500 lore.

1941

INDIANAPOLIS MOTOR SPEEDWAY

OFFICIAL
1941 PACEMAKER
INDIANAPOLIS
500 MILE SWEEPSTAKES
CHRYSLER

The Chrysler Newport paces the field to the green flag in 1941.

Chrysler officials with the 1941 Newport Pace Car.

LINCOLN

1946

When the cream-colored Lincoln cabriolet convertible led the 33-car field to Seth Klein's green flag, it was the culmination of months of hard work. Mr. Tony Hulman, Wilbur Shaw and the new Indianapolis Motor Speedway staff had wrought a miracle. Only scant months before, the speedway was a dilapidated facility, dodging a wrecking ball, while Shaw searched for someone with unflinching determination to purchase and rebuild the proud, old Brickyard. Thankfully, Mr. Hulman was that someone.

Our Lincoln Continental would be the last multi-cylinder (more than eight) car to pace the 500. The V-12 and V-16 engines were originally conceived, not for power, but smooth running, ease of transportation. Modern motor mounts and improved engineering techinques, made these engines obsolete.

Our pacemaker's V-12 displaced 305 cubic inches with a bore and stroke of 2.93 x 3.75 developing 130 horsepower at 3600 rpm. Compression was 7.20 to 1, drawing through a two-barrel Chandler-Grove carburetor. Except for dispensing with the old fork and blade connecting rod assembly, and a modern four bearing crankshaft, the cast iron L-head engine had changed little since Frank Johnson designed it. The V-12 was discontinued in 1948.

All the 1946 models were little more than warmed-over pre-war designs. In the eye pleasing Continental's case, that wasn't bad at all. There were only 201 of the two door cabriolets produced. The 125-inch wheelbase convertible, designated Model Number H66, is certainly a valued collector's item.

Our pace car driver was the new president of the Ford Motor Company, Henry Ford II. Mr. Ford had recently been named "outstanding young man of the year" by the Junior Chamber of Commerce. No doubt, he recalled the day his father, Edsel, paced the "greatest spectacle in racing."

For the second time since Tommy Milton proposed the tradition in 1936, a pace car was not awarded to the winner. In this case, popular 1946 Indy champ George Robson, met with an incident that echoed the experience of Mauri Rose and Floyd Davis in '41. "George did not receive a pace car," his brother Hal Robson explained. "He was to have received an oil painting of himself, and was awarded a trip to Italy, to tour the Ferrari plant," Hal recalled. "But I'm sure he never got the painting, and he was killed in a crash at Atlanta, just before he was to have left for Italy."

These are the only known occasions, when an Indy winner did not receive a pace car as part of his winnings.

1946

INDIANAPOLIS MOTOR SPEEDWAY

The 1946 Lincoln Continental Pace Car with Henry Ford II at the wheel. Speedway's new owner, Anton Hulman, Jr. in the back seat.

NASH AMBASSADOR

1947

When the name Nash is brought up in automotive conversations, one often thinks of his father or grandfather's rotund and rather hideous "bathtub on wheels" from the early '50s. Directly after World War II, however, Nash produced some really eye-catching designs.

After the huge, well appointed Lincoln pace car the previous year, the canary yellow and black Nash seemed a strange choice for pacemaker in 1947.

Two years before, Nash's president, George W. Mason had said: "Our car is the forerunner of cars to come."

Actually, Nash was on the cutting edge of something in America's future—economy in transportation. It was difficult, however, to interest the motoring public in a cheaply operating car, when gasoline was 17.9 cents per gallon.

Nash did not produce a convertible in '47, so their top of the line Ambassador four-door sedan did the honors. Our pacemaker's inline 6-cylinder had a bore and stroke of 3-3/8 x 4-3/8, measuring out to 234.8 cubic inches. Compression was 7.02 to 1. The crankshaft spun at a modest 3400 rpm, producing 112 horsepower.

Although the Nash was geared to economy, its 121 inch wheelbase chassis made the car surprisingly large and roomy.

George W. Mason was the driver of the pacemaker. He even persuaded screen star Clark Gable—a regular visitor to Indianapolis during the month of May—to pose with the car for photographers.

Apparently, the Nash appearing at the head of the 33-car field helped stimulate sales. A record 113,315 units were sold in '47, making the first instance of sales over 100,000 for the firm since the depression.

Eventually, Nash, along with Hudson, was absorbed into Rambler, and disappeared from the automotive scene.

Once again, the Indianapolis Motor Speedway had picked a car based on a revolutionary idea. It was just a little too far ahead of its time.

1947

1947 Nash Ambassador one of the few non-convertibles to pace the race.

CHEVROLET

1948

Chevrolet's very first car chosen as pacemaker, was the 1948 Stylemaster Six-Series. This body style was actually a holdover from 1942. But who could argue with success. The 1947 Chevrolet had been the number one selling car in America.

Our grey two-door convertible, from the 1500 FJ Series, was powered by an in-line 6-cylinder displacing 216.5 cubic inches with a bore and stroke of 3½ x 3¾. Horsepower was a modest 90 ponies at 3300 rpm. Compression was 6.5 to 1, pulling gasoline from a single barrel Carter carburetor. The solid valve lifters operated the overhead valves via pushrods and rocker arms. The crankshaft ran in four main bearings. Although the little "stovebolt" six dated back to 1937, it was a rugged, steady performer. Its basic design lasted until the early 1960s.

With a wheelbase of only 116-inches, the Stylemaster was the low priced sister to the Fleetline and Fleetmaster designs. A standard manual three-speed, was the only transmission offered.

Former three-time Indianapolis winner, and President of the Indianapolis Motor Speedway, Wilbur Shaw, was our pace car driver. Mr. Shaw was accompanied on the pace lap by Chevrolet Sales Manager, Mr. Thomas H. Keating.

1948

INDIANAPOLIS MOTOR SPEEDWAY

1948 Wilbur Shaw, 3-time winner and President of the IMS in the Chevrolet Fleetmaster 1948 Pace Car.

OLDSMOBILE "88"

1949

By 1948, Hudson was the performance car champ in America. To counteract this, Oldsmobile set out on an ambitious road that was to influence the automotive industry for years to come.

The new Olds V-8 engine, together with a completely different design from Cadillac, was the first modern, high compression, overhead valve V-8

The "Rocket Eight," together with the famous Futuramic styling, caused Indianapolis Motor Speedway officials to choose the GM product as pace car for 1949.

The "88" was actually a blend of old and new, suggested by Olds general manager, S.E. Skinner. The new V-8 engine in the older, smaller, but lighter "76" chassis, made the "88" a potent package. The resulting machine could more than hold its own on the tough NASCAR stock car circuit. "Make a date with a Rocket Eight," was an advertising slogan that swept the country. Later, the advertisment was changed to "Rocket 88".

Our pacemaker was powered by a 303.7 cubic inch V-8 engine with a bore and stroke of 3-3/4 x 3-7/16 producing 135 horsepower at 3600 rpm. Compression was 7.25 to 1. The overhead valves were operated by a camshaft deep in the V-shaped block. Hydraulic lifters, pushrods and rocker arms actuated the valves. This highly efficient, over-square engine was designed by Gilbert Burrell.

When the war ended, the old master of styling, Harley Earl, started working on a lithe, lower, more beautiful design. Mr. Earl was the guiding hand behind the entire Futuramic designs—including our "88".

As already stated, the 119.5-inch wheelbase chassis was identical to the older "76" frame. The "88" was slightly late getting to the market, but the wait was worth it.

Three-time 500 winner, Wilbur Shaw, accompanied by Oldsmobile's chief engineer, C.F. "Jack" Wolfram, wheeled the red convertible.

Wilbur felt the front row of Duke Nalon, Rex Mays and Jack McGrath jumped the start, passing the pacemaker over a hundred feet before the pit entrance. "Apparently, they felt 90 mph wasn't fast enough," Wilbur mused. Thereafter, Shaw left the pace car driving duties to others, while he waved the field into line, kneeling in the front passenger's seat, facing backward.

1949

Wilbur Shaw in the 1949 Olds "88", 1949.

OFFICIAL
PACE CAR
OLDSMOBILE '88'

STOP
OFFICIAL
PACE CAR
OLDSMOBILE "88"

MERCURY

1950

As a medium priced car, between Ford and Lincoln, the Mercury always seemed somewhat overlooked. Probably Mercury's biggest boost came from the movie screen. For years, lowered and channeled Mercs with flames painted back over the hood, were the rage in Hot Rod movies. Who could ever forget James Dean's Mercury in "Rebel Without A Cause?"

There was in 1950, however another pool of limelight awaiting the marque.

When the low, sleek, Mercury was selected as Indy Pace Car in 1950, Ford wasted no time in capitalizing on the advertising and extra prestige their product received. During the year, some 320,000 of the new models found a home, and the one-millionth Mercury was produced.

Our plush pacemaker was powered by a V-8 L-head engine of 255.4 cubic inches with a bore and stroke of 3.19 x 4. This "big brother" of Ford's cast iron wonder, produced 110 horsepower at 3600 rpm. The crankshaft was Ford's standard three main bearing unit. A Holley two-barrel carburetor fed fuel to the 6.80 to 1 compression pistons and heads.

The low-slung chassis had a wheelbase of 118-inches. The powertrain was a standard three-speed manual transmission, with column shift.

The logo of the winged god Mercury, appeared in the center of the letter "O" in the word "Official" on the pacemaker's doors. Power windows were a standard feature on all Mercury convertibles.

Benson Ford, head of the Lincoln-Mercury Division of the Ford Motor Company, served as pace car driver.

1950

Benson Ford, driver and Wilbur Shaw, passenger in the 1950 Mercury.

Wilbur Shaw, President of IMS with Benson Ford and the 1950 Pace Car.

1950 Mercury-Wilbur Shaw and Tony Hulman (front); Clark Gable and Barbara Stanwyck

CHRYSLER NEW YORKER

1951

With the exception of its restyled front end and slightly lower stance, the Virgil Exner designed 1951 New Yorker may have seemed very similar to its predecessors. Actually, it was quite different—at least mechanically. It was this mechanical difference that caused the New Yorker to be named as Indianapolis 500 pace car.

Our convertible was powered by a revolutionary Fire Power hemi-head V-8. The deep breathing configuration wasn't new. Offenhauser, Stutz and even Stoddard-Dayton had used the design. Basically, the work of W.E. Drinkard and M.L. Carpentier, it was, however, the first time a modern high compression passenger car engine had incorporated the design. The New Yorker displaced 331 cubic inches with an oversquare bore and stroke 4.81 x 3.63. The five main bearing crankshaft spun at 4000 rpm producing 180 horsepower. A Carter two-barrel carburetor fed the juice to the 7.5 to 1 compression heads. The hemi utilized the "slipper" piston arrangement, where the piston "crouched" down between the crankshaft counterweights at the bottom of each stroke. The complex overhead valve system required four rocker arms and eight sets of intake and exhaust pushrods and rocker arms.

This impressive engine would influence V-8 design for years to come, and would be a major cause of the horsepower race during the next two decades.

The 131.5-inch wheelbase chassis was a holdover from previous years. Its independent coil front and leaf rear springs had the bumps controlled by the new Oriflow shock absorbers. The Hydraguide power steering, later known simply as full-time, was the first of its kind.

Chrysler declared they were building the "Finest Engineered Cars in the World." One thing for sure, they were on the cutting edge of engine technology.

Our pacemaker was proudly driven by Crysler Division President Dave Wallace.

1951

INDIANAPOLIS MOTOR SPEEDWAY

LAP No
CAR No
OFFICIAL PACE CAR
CHRYSLER
500 MILE RACE
MAY 30 1951
FirePower
487 M 2

Wilbur Shaw and Chyrsler official in the 1951

Wilbur Shaw and his passenger in 1951 Chrysler.

FAMOUS

Walter P. Chrysler examines a model of the ill-fated Airflow. (Courtesy of the Chrysler Historical Collection)

Elwood Engel (Courtesy Chrysler Historical Collection)

E.L. Cord
(Courtesy of Auburn-Cord-Duesenberg Museum)

Johnny Aitken at the wheel of his Peugeot. (Courtesy of Phil Harms Photo Collection)

C.W. Van Ranst

FOLKS

(L to R) Henry Ford, Arthur C. Newby, Frank Wheeler, Carl G. Fisher and James Allison.

Arthur C. Newby

Carroll Shelby, 1987 Indy Pace Car driver. (Courtesy of Chyrsler Motor Corp.)

STUDEBAKER

1952

"The name Studebaker is synonymous with dependable land transportation. And, it is significant that of the more than 100 makes of cars once produced in Indiana, only Studebaker remains." With these words, Wilbur Shaw announced the Studebaker Commander V-8 as pace car for the 1952 Indianapolis 500.

It was also the firm's centennial year as a producer of vehicles and the golden anniversary of the automotive division.

Our convertible was powered by a 232.6 cubic inch engine with a bore and stroke of 3-3/8 x 3-1/4. The drop forged steel crankshaft ran in five main bearings, twisting out 120 horespower at 4000 rpm. A compression ratio of 7.0 to 1 drew fuel from a two-barrel Stromberg carburetor. Overhead valves were actuated by pushrods and rocker arms from an in block camshaft. Valve lifters were the solid type.

The surprisingly smooth ride given by the relatively short—for those days—115-inch wheelbase chassis, was outstanding. Suspension was the usual independent coil front, semi-elliptic leaf rear, backed up by Houde-Monroe shocks.

The styling was by the renowned Raymond Loewy, often lauded as an automotive artist. While the design was reminiscent of the ill-fated Tucker, it was distinctively Studebaker.

At first, Studebaker president and chairman of the board Harold Vance was announced as pace car driver. When he declined, executive vice-president P.O. Peterson accepted the honor. As always, Wilbur Shaw accompanied Mr. Peterson on the pace lap.

1952

OFFICIAL PACE CAR
STUDEBAKER
500 MILE RACE MAY 30, 1952

OFFICIAL PACE CAR
STUDEBAKER
INDIANA
BJ 4036

FORD

1953

In commemoration of the Ford Motor Company's Fiftieth Anniversary, the Indianapolis Motor Speedway chose the Ford Sunliner as the 1953 pace car.

Our pacemaker was powered by the last of the venerable flathead V-8 engines. The 239 cubic inch cast iron L-head had a bore and stroke of 3.19 x 3.75 with a compression ratio of 7.2 to 1. This produced 110 horsepower at 3800 rpm. The crankshaft turned in three main bearings, and a Holley two-barrel carburetor fed the gas.

The beautifully turned out 115-inch wheelbase convertible used a Ford-O-Matic automatic transmission to transfer power to the road. By this juncture, Ford had long since gone to independent front suspension.

The pace car sported fender skirts, chrome rocker moldings, a continental spare tire mount, special crossed checkered flags on each front fender and official pace car lettering. The spotless paint finish was called "Pace Car White." The top was white orlon with a matching boot cover. The interior was Anniversary Gold, Pearlescent White and black. The dash, top bows and any trim were painted Anniversary Gold. The actual pace car stands out from its sister cars, because of its special wire wheels, thought to be a Firestone promotion. The replicas had regular steel wheels and full wheelcovers.

Besides the actual pace car, Ford produced 2,000 replicas as a display car for their dealers during May. The car became so popular, many dealers produced several "fake" pace cars to sell. Sunliner sales for 1953, were 40,861 units.

The 1953 500-mile race winner, Bill Vukovich, received a replica pace car. The original pacemaker is on display in the Henry Ford Museum.

William C. Ford became the fourth member of his family to drive the pace car.

1953

OFFICIAL
PACE CAR
500 MILE RACE MAY 30 1953

83 88 92 97 98
FORD
OFFICIAL
PACE CAR
500 MILE RACE MAY 30 1953

Tony Hulman and William Clay Ford with the 1953 Ford Sunliner.

DODGE

1954

The initial appearance of Dodge as pace car came in 1954. The Indianapolis Motor Speedway honored the marque on its fortieth anniversary. Although Chryslers had served as pacemaker several times, it marked the first time any MoPar subsidiary lines had made the grade.

Our pace car was powered by the Red Ram hemi-head V-8 displacing 241 cubic inches with a bore and stroke of 3.312 x 3.25. The compression ratio was 7.5 to 1, and with the special Offenhauser intake manifold and Rochester four-barrel carb, gave 170 horsepower at 4400 rpm. The crankshaft was a five main bearing design. Solid valve lifters were employed to control valve float.

Although Chrysler never quoted an exact horsepower rating for this engine, W.C. "Bill" Newberg, president of Dodge Division, was quoted several times, giving the 170 horsepower figure as the optimum output.

The Dodge Royal's wheelbase was only 114-inches, making it one of the smallest pacemakers in many years.

In honor of being selected pace car, Dodge renamed 701 of its line—already known as the V-8 Royal Series—to Royal 500 convertible. The pace car replicas sold for $2632. These stylish machines carried the same equipment as the actual pace car, including a Continental-style rear spare tire mount, Kelsey-Hayes wire wheels, special trim and lettering. If you had the patience to wait, and wanted an exact pace car replica, you could order the special manifold and carburetor. This gave the standard V-8 a 20 horsepower increase.

Mr. W.C. Newberg served as pace car driver.

As usual, Wilbur Shaw made sure the 33 chargers behind the pace car stayed in line. In was Wilbur's last 500-mile race.

On October 30, 1954, Mr. Shaw, one of racing's greatest friends and ambassadors, died in the crash of a light plane.

It is interesting to note that on June 16, 1954, a Dodge Royal 500 convertible paced a special match race, dedicating Chrysler's new proving grounds at Chelsea, Michigan. Whether or not this was the same car that paced the Indianapolis 500, has been lost to time. If so, then Bill Vukovich, Sr. received a replica pace car two years straight.

The Chelsea event was won by Jack McGrath, over Troy Ruttman, Vukovich and Jimmy Bryan.

1954

INDIANAPOLIS MOTOR SPEEDWAY

1954 Dodge with Dean Martin and Jerry Lewis aboard.

Dean Martin and Jerry Lewis in the 1954 Dodge.

Indianapolis
500 MILE RACE MAY 31st 1954
DODGE
Official
PACE CAR

CHEVROLET

1955

In 1955, Chevrolet manufacturing manager, Edward N. Cole, brought about changes that shook the automotive world. Mr. Cole was the central figure behind the sensationally popular "55 Chevy Bel Air.

Its wonderful clean styling soon caused Indianapolis 500 officials to announce Cole's "baby" as pace car.

Our Bel Air pacemaker was powered by a 265 cubic inch V-8 with a bore and stroke of 3.75 x 3.00 and 8.0 to 1 compression. This particular engine was the "Power Pack" version, producing 180 horsepower. The 18 horse jump from the regular engine was due to a Rochester four-barrel carburetor. This overhead valve engine was famous for its light weight. The stamped-metal rocker arms, hollow pushrods and splash lubrication system eliminated separate oil feeder lines and rocker arm shafts, saving a great deal of weight. Even more weight was saved by the pressed forged steel five main bearing crankshaft. Pressed-in piston pins eliminated the old slitted rod and locking bolt.

The engine design was the work of several men. Cole was assisted by Edward H. "Crankshaft" Kelly and Harry F. Barr. The latter, borrowed from Cadillac. A new weight saving block casting technique came from John Dolza of GM's Central Engineering Staff. The revolutionary overhead valve idea was originated by Clayton B. Leach of Pontiac.

The engine, known as the "Turbo-Fire," was so successful, it survives, in one form or another, to this very day.

The 115-inch wheelbase chassis, designed by Barr, was 18 percent lighter, but 50 percent stiffer than past Chevrolet frames. The "spherical-joint" independent front suspension employed unequal upper and lower A-arms. Bounce was controlled by double-action shocks, running down through coil springs. The familiar live axle and semi-elliptic leaf springs handled the torque from the new open drive shaft.

The attractive body was designed by Clare MacKichan, Charles A. Stebbins and Carl H. Renner, under the guidance of the legendary Harley Earl.

Thomas H. Keating was at the wheel of the beautiful red and white convertible. Mr. Keating had ridden on the pace lap with Wilbur Shaw in 1948. Mr. Tony Hulman took over the traffic direction duties from the front seat. The job formerly done by the late Wilbur Shaw.

A cut out in the trunk lid allowed a movie camera to photograph the racers on the pace lap.

Once again, Chevy was America's best selling car, producing some 1.7 million, while capturing 44 percent of the low-price car market.

1955

27
» CHEVROLET «
500
INDIANAPOLIS
MOTOR
SPEEDWAY
MAY 30
1955
OFFICIAL PACE CAR
500 MILE RACE

CHEVROLET
OFFICIAL
BX 4107

Dinah Shore rides in the Chevy Pace Car during pre-race activities in 1955.

Front row drivers: (L to R) Jerry Hoyt, Jack McGrath & Tony Bettenhausen in the '55 Chevy.

1955 Pace Cars lined up in the pits.

Mauri Rose, '41, '47 & '48 winner standing with 1955 Pace Car. Driver: Chevy Official; Passenger: Tony Hulman.

DESOTO

1956

Hernando de Soto was a great explorer and adventurer, who pushed back the horizons of man's world and ideas.

No doubt, he would have approved of his four wheel namesake, designed by Chrysler's trendsetting Virgil Exner. If so, he would have especially been proud of the white and gold (gilded may be a better description) convertible which paced the '56 Hoosier classic.

In February of that year, Chrysler introduced the sensational Hemi-powered DeSoto Adventurer. This amazing 341 cubic inch brute delivered 320 horsepower at 5200 rpm. An Adventurer blasted down Daytona's sandy beach at 137.293 mph. At Chrysler's Chelsea Proving Grounds, a second machine turned a lap of the banked oval at over 144 mph.

Adventurer's marks were not confined only to the track. Nearly a thousand of the potent machines were sold in a six week period.

It didn't take long for Indy Pace Car people to notice the impression DeSoto was making on the market.

There was only one problem. The Adventurer was only produced in a two-door hardtop model. This was long before hatch roofs. So a Fireflite convertible, dressed up in the Adventurer's gleaming gold colors, was sent to Indy.

Our DeSoto pacemaker was powered by the Fireflite Hemi-head V-8 displacing 330.4 cubic inches with a bore and stroke of 3.72 x 3.80. A Carter four-barrel carburetor fed gasoline to 8.5 to 1 compression heads producing 255 horsepower at 4400 rpm. Chrysler had solved a great deal of the valve float inherent in earlier Hemis, allowing the DeSoto to use hydraulic valve lifters. The familiar five main bearing MoPar crankshaft was more than adequate.

This was a year before Chrysler went to torsion bar front suspension, so the DeSoto still had coils up front, leaf springs at the rear. The actual pace car was equipped with heavy duty suspension and Oriflow shock absorbers. The powerful engine could spin the 760 x 15 tires with ease. This was the first year for the push-button Powerflite automatic transmission.

Brakes were the Bendix double shoe, twin-wheel cylinder type. A good, but touchy brake—at least until the driver became used to them. In an era prior to disc brakes, they were exactly what this 4300 pound, 126-inch wheelbase car needed.

The steering was just as quick as the brakes. The full-time power steering made the car easy to handle, even in the closest parking spaces.

A camera was mounted in the trunk of our pacemaker, and shot movie footage through a square cut in the rear of the trunk lid.

Chrysler was just beginning their successful tail fin design. They had not yet gone to the extremely high fin, later incorporated into all their cars.

Dapper Irvin Woolson, President of the DeSoto Division, was driver of the pace car. He later described it as "the thrill of my life".

A few hours later, Pat Flaherty received the keys to our beauty.

The DeSoto was a classic pace car of the 1950's. Certainly one, if not the best looking pacemaker of the decade. Officially, about 100 "Pacesetter" convertibles, sans the "Official Pace Car" lettering, were offered to the public at $3615 per unit. For some reason, there were a few replicas produced in various color combinations, with the lettering.

The marque never before, nor ever again, would pace Indy. Chrysler discontinued the DeSoto line in 1961.

1956

INDIANAPOLIS MOTOR SPEEDWAY

L.I. Woolson, driver and Tony Hulman pace the race in 1956 in the DeSoto Adventurer.

LAP No
CAR No
INDIANAPOLIS 500 MILE RACE, MAY 30, 1956
PACE

DESOTO SETS THE PACE

MERCURY

1957

The fresh, new styling of the 1957 Mercury, influenced Indianapolis Motor Speedway officials to select the racy convertible as pace car.

Our sleek Turnpike Cruiser was powered by a V-8 engine displacing 368 cubic inches with a bore and stroke of 4 x 3.65 producing 290 horsepower at 4600 rpm. The overhead valves were operated via the conventional in block camshaft, utilizing the hydraulic lifters, pushrod and rocker arm setup. The crankshaft was a completely counterbalanced, five main bearing design. A Holley four-barrel carburetor fed premium gasoline to the potent 9.70 to 1 high compression engine.

This was the most powerful pace car, up to that time, in Indianapolis history. It would, however, be surpassed nearly every year for the next decade.

The 122-inch wheelbase machine, equipped with 8.50 x 14 tires, appeared to be the lowest, widest pacemaker of them all.

F.C. "Jack" Reith, general manager of Mercury and vice president of the Ford Motor Company, was our pace car driver.

This was the first year for the new $100,000 control Tower, Tower Terrace seats and 1,300 foot pit area.

It was also the first year for the pace car to lead the field for two laps. A parade, or form up lap, was added to the usual pace circuit. Race cars were to exit the new pit area single file, forming the customary eleven rows of three cars on the first lap. During this lap, Eddie Russo and Elmer George collided, eliminating their cars from the race.

The race was won by veteran Sam Hanks, destined to become a six-time Indy Pace Car driver.

Of all the pacemakers he drove, Sam liked the Mercury he won the best of all. "It was powerful, easy to drive and really handled well," Sam recalls.

Hanks sold his pace car about two years after winning the race. He lost track of it for a while, but sees it every now and then on the west coast. "Whoever owns it, now," according to Sam, "has it in great shape." So, although the present owner is unknown, at least we know one of the '50's pace cars is still around.

1957

1957 Mercury Pace Car with the 500 Festival Queen.

INDIANAPOLIS MOTOR SPEEDWAY RADIO NETWORK
INDIANAPOLIS 50
MAY 30, 1957
INDIANAPOLIS 500-MILE RACE
MERCURY
OFFICIAL
PACE CAR

PONTIAC

1958

By 1958, Pontiac was the only modern day General Motors marque never selected as pace car.

With the inroads the storming Bonnevilles were making into the NASCAR stock car ranks, and this was GM's fiftieth anniversary, Indianapolis Motor Speedway officals hastened to change this.

Our Bonneville convertible, with its sculptured side panels, was powered by an overhead valve V-8 displacing 370 cubic inches with a bore and stroke of 4.06 x 3.56. This particular Bonneville was equipped with an optional Rochester fuel injection unit. This performance package also included 10.5 to 1 cylinder heads and a high-lift camshaft, producing 310 horsepower at 4800 rpm. The block was cast iron, and the crankshaft ran in five main bearings. The valves were actuated by Clayton B. Leach's stamped-metal rocker arms, hollow pushrods and splash lubricating system.

There were only about 200 of these fuel injected engines produced. Just enough, in those days, for NASCAR certification as a stock production engine.

The well appointed and chrome trimmed "rag top" was carried by a 122-inch wheelbase frame, with coil springs fore and aft. A Hydra-Matic transmission was standard fare.

Oddly enough, the Bonneville pace car was not a factory, but a dealer backed project.

After his fantastic victory in the 1957 Indianapolis 500, Sam Hanks retired from racing. Sam served his first term as pace car driver in '58.

This was the second year for the cars to leave the pit area single file, then form up in their eleven rows of three on the track. The front row, consisting of Dick Rathmann, Ed Elisian and Jimmy Reece, left the pit area ahead of the pace car. They had to go all the way around, and get back into position before the green flag dropped. When Hanks pulled the pace car off the track, the flagman kept the yellow flag out. By the following lap, the front row cars had pulled into position. The green was out, and the race was on. A multi-car crash on the north turn, of the first lap, claimed the life of popular Pat O'Connor. Many of the top cars were eliminated. Jimmy Bryan was the eventual winner.

Although the miscue by the front frow starters in no way contributed to the tragic accident, the cars were no longer started from the pit area after 1958. Thus, ending two years of confusion on the start.

1958

Shirley MacLaine waving to the fans from the 1958 Pontiac Bonneville Pace Car.

Sam Hanks driving the 1958 Pontiac.

1958 Pontiac Bonneville driven by Sam Hanks, '57 winner. Tony Hulman and passenger in the back seat.

BUICK ELECTRA 225

1959

When this handsome Electra 225 was chosen, exactly twenty years had passed since Buick's initial debut as a pace car.

A great many things had changed. "It doesn't really look like a Buick," was a phrase often heard. For one thing, the portholes were gone. That was only a small part of it, however.

The "Delta Wing" design fins, together with a great deal of chrome, mark this brilliant white "Deuce and a Quarter" as a fitting end to the 1950's. The design was highly regarded then, but considered somewhat garish today. "Beauty is in the eye of the beholder," may be said of this well engineered creation, mostly from the drawing board of Harley Earl.

Horsepower was a big market stick in '59, and this powerful overhead valve example filled the bill. The 401 cubic inch V-8 "nail head" produced 325 horses at 4400 rpm. The five main bearing crankshaft featured a bore and stroke of 4.1875 x 3.64. The 10.5 to 1 compression made premium fuel mandatory. A four-barrel carburetor, either Carter or Rochester, fed this formidable cast iron engine. This series of engines was one of the quietest high compression overhead valve V-8s ever produced. The pushrod and rocker arm setup was exceptionally tight, and the rather narrow heads drained the oil back to the crankcase quickly. You seldom ever saw one of these engines pumping oil through their valve seals. The large valves were positioned straight up and down, hence the term "nail head."

A smooth "Shiftless" Dynaflow transmission, coupled with a soft, but stable ride, put this 126.3-inch wheelbase over the bricks with hardly a ripple.

Sam Hanks, in his second straight year as a pace car driver, did the honors. That is, when he could get Mr. Hulman from behind the wheel of this 1950's classic.

1959

Tony Hulman and passengers in the 1959 Buick Electra.

Rodger Ward and his wife in the 1959 Buick Electra 225 Pace Car.

Rodger Ward and his wife.

OLDSMOBILE "98"

1960

The completely restyled low, sleek Oldsmobile Ninety-Eight was pace car for the 1960 Indianapolis 500.

Our pacemaker was powered by a cast iron overhead valve V-8 displacing 394 cubic inches with a bore and stroke of 4-1/8 x 3-11/16 inches. The 10.0 to 1 compression heads and Multi-jet Rochester 4GC four-barrel carburetor, helped the over-square engine to develop 315 horsepower at 4600 rpm.

A surprisingly quick "Jetaway" Hydra-Matic transmission helped this 4412 pound 126.3-inch wheelbase convertible punch to an easy 120 mph. While the acceleration was rapid, the stopping was just as fast. Super-wide drum power brakes made for sure, safe stops, on "fat" 9.00 x 14 tubeless tires.

Courtesy lights, padded dash and wheel trim rings were standard equipment. The actual pace car was upholstered in leather.

Some 7,284 of the Ninety-Eight five passenger convertibles were produced.

The pace car was supplied to the Speedway through local Indianapolis dealer, Charlie Stuart Oldsmobile.

Sam Hanks reprised his roll as pace car driver.

This 500-mile race has been called the greatest 500 of them all. An early race duel between Jim Rathmann, Rodger Ward and Troy Ruttman set the tempo for the full distance. Ruttman's car failed and Rathmann and Ward duelled, and swapped positions almost to the checkered flag. Worn tires finally slowed Ward, and Rathmann won a well deserved victory—and the beautiful Olds convertible.

1960

Tony Hulman with Olds Representatives in 1960 Pace Car.

THE INDIANAPOLIS NEWS
Louis BAUMAN
75
Kokomo, Ind.

"500" FESTIVAL
SHOP

FORD THUNDERBIRD

1961

In 1961, a gilded Ford Thunderbird led the field to the starter's flag. For the Fiftieth Anniversary of the world's greatest race, what better color could the pace car be?

By race day, Thunderbird sales had already reached 50,000. Sales ultimately totaled 73,051 units, with 10,516 of them convertibles.

Our T-Bird was powered by an overhead valve V-8 displacing 390 cubic inches with a bore and stroke of 4.05 x 3.75. Turning the five main bearing crankshaft at 4600 rpm produced 300 horsepower. Fuel was delivered to the 9.6 to 1 compression pistons via a Holley four-barrel carburetor.

"Unique in All the World" was a Ford styling slogan that certainly befit the Thunderbird.

Bill Boyer, working under vice-president of styling George Walker, designed our pacemaking beauty. The plush, white leather interior was the work of Art Querfeld. Stuart Fry designed the "Swing-Away" steering wheel. This unique device allowed the wheel to be moved ten inches laterally to the right for the driver's ease of entry and exit from the comfortable bucket seat.

The T-Bird was certainly the finest riding and handling 113-inch wheelbase car in America, if not the world. The coil sprung front suspension system was completely different from any other design. The coil springs were located above the upper wishbones, while the lower control arm was a single rigid bar. A strut ran from its outer end to a rubber bushing mounted to the body. The rear featured leaf springs with the forward mounts in rubber bushings. This allowed the wheel to move backward and forward as well as up and down. The T-Bird actually stepped over the bumps. This was an old ploy used by Mercedes-Benz to soften the choppy ride of short wheelbase cars. Ford revived and improved this technique to the highest degree possible.

While the Thunderbird was still in a sports car mode, it was—at 4130 pounds—far from being a lightweight machine.

A much quicker steering ratio was used to enhance handling, and new larger brakes added increased stopping power. A three-speed Ford-O-Matic transmission transferred the power to the rear wheels.

Sam Hanks, back for a fourth straight year as a pace car driver, wheeled this low-slung, golden and chrome beauty.

When one young Indy driver spied his mother admiring the pace car, he promised to win it for her. After an effort of some 3 hours, 35 minutes, 37.49 seconds, A.J. Foyt made good his word.

1961

Photo Shop employee, Marilyn Scott poses with the 1961 T-Bird Pace Car.

Lorne Greene and Dan Blocker from the hit TV show Bonanza ride in the 1961 T-Bird in the pre-race activities.

Tony Hulman with the 1961 T-Bird.

STUDEBAKER LARK

1962

The radical styling of Raymond Loewy's Studebaker Avanti caused the Indianapolis Motor Speedway to name it pace car for 1962. Unfortunately, the Avanti was not put into production soon enough, and the compact Studebaker Lark was named honorary pace car. A prototype Avanti did make an appearance on race day, taking a single lap with the two-man Studebaker Indy cars.

At this point in time, Studebaker was the only marque to serve as pace car four times.

The Lark Daytona convertible was powered by an overhead valve V-8 of 289 cubic inches with a bore and stroke of 3-9/16 x 3-5/8 producing 210 horsepower at 4500 rpm. Compression was 8.5 to 1, and the crankshaft ran in five main bearings. Solid lifters, pushrods and rocker arms gave the valve action.

With its nimble 113-inch wheelbase chassis, the Lark was fun to drive and possessed surprising performance.

The unitized body and the V-8 into an economy compact car, was sneered at by many automotive engineers of the day. As in the case with Studebaker so many times before, the larger companies were soon to copy the "Studbuster's" ideas and innovations. Dart, Valiant, Comet, Falcon, Chevy II, Tempest and other compacts would soon sport V-8 engines.

Sam Hanks was back for his fifth straight time as pace car driver.

Some time after the 500-mile race, winner Rodger Ward accepted the keys to a new Avanti. According to press releases, Rodger was the first private owner of this advanced sports car.

Even with all the hoopla, pace car publicity and excitement about the Avanti, Studebaker was facing insurmountable financial problems. The venerable company closed its South Bend, Indiana plant in '63, moving to Canada. The last Studebaker came off the line in 1966. After 114 years of pride and accomplishment, it was all over.

J.M. Studebaker had long been quoted: "always give more than you promise." Apparently, the statement was taken out of context. The continuation of his statement was, "but don't give too much or you will go broke."

Perhaps these final words of wisdom were Studebaker Corporation's epitaph.

1962

Tony Hulman with local Studebaker dealer, Charlie Stewart.

1962 Studebaker Lark Daytona with Speedway owner Tony Hulman and Indy Stude dealer Charlie Stewart.

CHRYSLER "300"

1963

By 1963, long-time Chrysler stylist Virgil Exner had been replaced by Elwood Engel. While Engel cleaned up the Chrysler's lines, he also retained many of Exner's pet designs. The huge, inverted trapezoid shaped grilles; large, open wheel wells; bulging "bug-eyed" headlamp housings and creased body sides were holdovers from the 1962 models. Engel's major change was the sparse use of chrome. Chrysler's new "Crisp, Clean, Custom Look" drew a great deal of press attention.

One of the sharpest models of the breed, was the two-door Chrysler "300" Sport Series convertible. The "300" Series had always stood for performance, and Indianapolis Motor Speedway officials chose the stylish machine to lead the field over the starting line on Memorial Day.

The engine in this particular pace car has caused quite a dilemma. Given Chrysler's earlier predilection for special cars and assorted engine combinations, exact identification was, to say the least, difficult.

First of all, the standard "300", excluding the "J" series, was equipped with a 383 cubic inch engine. It's also been listed as a 361 incher, with various horsepower ratings including, 305, 340, 360 and 365.

After painstaking research, we believe the actual pace car was powered by a cast iron overhead valve V-8 displacing 413 cubic inches with a bore and stroke of 4.188 x 3.750. The 10.0 to 1 compression engine produced 360 horsepower at 4800 rpm. The horsepower figure makes for more confusion, since a stock 413, with a single four-barrel carburetor produced 340 ponies. The 360 horsepower figure leads us to believe our pacemaker was equipped with the optional twin Carter four-barrel carburetor setup. The crankshaft was the usual five main bearing unit. It's believed this particular engine was equipped with solid valve lifters. The normal pushrod and rocker arm arrangement operated the valves.

A push-button three-speed Torqueflite automatic transmission handled the punch, while 11-inch self-adjusting power drum brakes put the stop on the 122-inch wheelbase beauty. Front suspension was the reliable torsion bar and A-arm setup, with conventional leaf springs at the rear.

The "300" received some quizzical glances from veteran race drivers and railbirds. The exterior was painted metallic turquoise, with white lettering. In a certain light, or photographic angle, the car looked positively green! It really wasn't, but the exact color was never used on another Indy Pace Car.

The interior was done in white leather, with rich turquoise fabrics and matching carpet covered the floor and door panels. The "300" carried four individual bucket seats, with the front two, power adjustable. Electric power windows and power steering were standard features.

The pace car created such a stir, that Chrysler, ever sensative to public interest, produced 1,861 replica convertibles, and 306 two-door hardtop coupes based on the "300" Sport Series. Powered by the 383, these popular machines were known as the Pace Setter Series, and commemorated Chrysler's participation at Indy.

For the sixth straight and final time, popular 1957 Indy winner Sam Hanks drove the pace car. This broke the record of five straight, held by IMS founder Carl G. Fisher. Jim Rathmann is the only other driver to pace Indy six times. Jim's appearances, however, were not consecutive.

1963

INDIANAPOLIS MOTOR SPEEDWAY

1963 Festival car in pits.

Harlan Fengler, Chief Steward of the 500 in the 1963 Chrysler 300.

FORD MUSTANG

1964

1964

On April 17, 1964, Ford Motor Company dropped a bombshell on the automotive scene. The Mustang—oft referred to as a 1964 ½ model— combined young, new sculptured styling with performance and affordability. The styling was so sleek and fresh, it won the Tiffany Award for Excellence in American Design. The only car ever so honored.

The dream of an eight man team headed by Lee Iococca, the Mustang owed its clean styling to Joe Oros, Gail Halderman and David Ash.

Within a matter of days, following its introduction, the Mustang had captured the hearts of Americans, and the attention of Indianapolis Motor Speedway officials. It was quickly named as pace car for the 1964 500-mile race.

Our Wimbleton White two-door convertible was powered by an overhead valve V-8 displacing 289 cubic inches with a bore and stroke of 4.00 x 2.87. The Challenger high-performance engine produced 271 horsepower at an astounding 6000 rpm. The drop forged steel camshaft and solid valve lifters operated valves via a pushrod rocker arm stetup similar to the small block Chevy. The 10.5 to 1 compression engine took its premium fuel from a model "K" Ford four-barrel carburetor.

Weight saving was a big part of this engine. Engineer George F. Stirrat's little engine block was so short in height, it only extended as far as the crankshaft's centerline. The block was so small it didn't even leave room for entire counterweighting of the five main bearing crankshaft. Here, Mr. Stirrat borrowed an idea from our 1925 Rickenbacker pacemaker. One weight was cast as part of the flywheel, while another was cast into the front pulley adaptor.

It would have been all for naught, if not for Harold C. Grant's nodular-iron castings and shell-molding process using resin-filled cores. A Ford employee since '32, Mr. Grant's techinques sent many engineers back to their drawing boards.

The basic concept of this engine had already powered Jim Clark's Lotus—Ford to a second place finish in the '63 500-miler.

A four-speed transmission, standard for the 271 horsepower engine, sent torque to a limited-slip differential. The 108-inch wheelbase chassis was basically from the Falcon.

With a judicious mix of Falcon and Fairlane parts, and a completely new size and type American car, Ford was able to hold the base price of a Mustang to $2368.

Sales figures had been projected at 100,000 cars for the first year. A saturation of advertising, however, coupled with exposure as the Indianapolis 500 pace car just after public introduction, equaled this figure in the first four months! Ford sold 263,434 Mustangs, 28,833 of them convertibles, in '64. On April 17, 1965, its first birthday, the "Stang" had sold over 418,000 cars! The nearly unchanged 1965 model helped the marque over the one-million production figure in just 24 months. It was an unprecedented achievement.

After a fourteen year absence as pace car driver, Mr. Benson Ford drove this sensational machine.

Harlan Fengler in the 1964½ Mustang Pace Car.

Pace Car and the field on race day!

A restored Mustang Pace Car now resides in the Indianapolis Motor Speedway Hall of Fame Museum.

PLYMOUTH FURY

1965

Walter P. Chrysler's popular Plymouth, designed as an economy car in 1928, did not appear as an Indy Pace Car until 1965. To this date, the beautifully styled two-door Sport Fury convertible, is the only example of the marque to be so honored.

Plymouth, Chrysler's long-time champion of the compact car, produced a stunning, restyled machine. The Fury III rivaled its big brother Chrysler in appearance, size, quality and performance.

It's a cinch Richard Petty's performance on the NASCAR circuit in 1963 and '64, at the wheel of his blue Plymouth, didn't do any harm to MoPar's image. "King Richard" claimed 14 of Plymouth's 19 victories in '63, and wheeled his familiar Hemi powered number 43 to the NASCAR title the following year.

It was more than enough to warm the heart of Chrysler's racing boss. Namely, the great former midget driving champ and Indy veteran Ronney Householder. Rest assured the outspoken "House" never let anyone forget what Plymouth had accomplished, and the division received constant national attention. No doubt, this helped to influence officials, when pace car time rolled around.

Our popular pace car was powered by the "Commando" 383 cubic inch V-8 with a bore and stroke of 4.250 x 3.375. This consistent performer produced 270 horsepower at 4400 rpm. This particular engine had a compression ratio of 9.20 to 1. A Carter two-barrel carburetor delivered the fuel. The counterbalanced steel crankshaft ran in five main bearings. The overhead valve acton was induced via the usual pushrod and rocker arm arrangement.

A Torqueflite three-speed automatic transmission sent power to Goodyear 8.25 x 14 whitewall tires. With 390 pounds of torque under the driver's foot, it was no trouble to "chirp the skins" on take off.

As already stated, this was one of the largest cars Plymouth had ever turned out. The 119-inch wheelbase helped the Fury ride like a much more expensive car. This was also due to the outstanding characteristics of the torsion bar front suspension, and long leaf springs at the rear. In the author's opinion, this particular model Plymouth possessed one of the finest balanced suspension systems ever produced by MoPar. It was solid, but demonstrated much better than average ride, with none of the heavy chop sometimes encountered with a firm suspension.

The 11-inch power-assisted drum brakes were standard fare front and rear.

Our pace car's white exterior was further enhanced by a blue convertible top and matching vinyl interior.

Inside, the five-passenger Sport Fury featured front bucket seats, and a console mounted floor shift. For the first time since 1956, Chrysler products were no longer equipped with pushbutton transmission selectors. This was also Plymouth's first year for curved side windowglass.

This was an extremely fine year for Plymouth sales, which stood at 728,288 units for the calendar year. Through the '65 model year, the division's sales figures averaged nearly 370,000 cars annually. Mr. Chrysler would have been proud.

Chrysler-Plymouth general manager, Mr. P.N. Buckminster, was our pace car driver.

The race was won by Jim Clark's rear-engine Lotus-Ford, sounding the death rattle for the roadster. Thus, Clark became the first foreign driver to receive an Indy Pace Car as a prize.

1965

INDIANAPOLIS MOTOR SPEEDWAY

1965 Chief Steward of the 500 Harlan Fengler and the Plymouth Fury.

1965 Pace Lap.

500
INDIANAPOLIS MOTOR SPEEDWAY
500
OFFICIAL
Plymouth
PACE CAR
FORTY-NINTH ANNUAL INDIANAPOLIS 500 MILE RACE · MAY 31, 1965

MERCURY COMET CYCLONE GT

1966

"Indianapolis officials do not select their pace cars lightly. They look to a leader like Mercury Comet, the one that's repeatedly proved leadersip. This, Mercury Comet has in spades and cubes and records—a heritage of more world's records, in fact, than any other U.S. make." This is a direct quote from Mercury advertisments that graced newspapers and magazines, heralding the Comet Cyclone GT as Indy's choice as pace car in '66.

Our red beauty was powered by an overhead valve V-8 displacing 390 cubic inches with a bore and stroke combination of 4.05 x 3.78 producing 335 horsepower at 4800 rpm. A Ford four-barrel carburetor provided premium fuel for this 10.5 to 1 compression engine. The crankshaft ran in five main bearings. Hydraulic valve lifters operated the valves through a pushrod rocker arm arrangement.

Ford's chief engineer, Robert Stevenson, designed this engine to replace the old Y-block. The potent 390 was a member of the FE or "big block" Ford family of engines.

The 116-inch wheelbase Cyclone GT was equipped with twin hood scoops, heavy duty suspension, a power transfer rear axle, dual exhausts, four-on-the-floor transmission shifter and chrome center mag wheels.

Thanks to the white leather bucket seats and interior, the brilliant red exterior with white body stripe trim, looked extra sharp.

Only 2,158 Cyclone GT convertibles were produced during the year.

Super Stock Magazine named the GT "Performance Car of the Year."

Mr. Benson Ford was back for his third time as pace car driver.

1966

INDIANAPOLIS MOTOR SPEEDWAY

1966 Pace Lap.

Official PACE CAR
Mercury COMET
CYCLONE GT
INDIANAPOLIS 500

Harlan Fengler with the '65 Mercury Comet Cyclon GT.

CHEVROLET CAMARO

Chevrolet, constantly looking for an affordable sports car, produced the first Camaro for 1967. The racy little five passenger pony car was soon tabbed as Indy's pace car.

The Camaro SS (Super Sport) was powered by an L78 396 cubic inch V-8 with a bore and stroke of 4.094 x 3.76. Since the pacemaker and three backup cars were modified by the Chevrolet Experimental Department, no exact horsepower figures are available. In stock form the big block L78 put out 375 horsepower at 4800 rpm. The cast nodular iron crankshaft ran in five steel-backed bearings. The forged alloy steel connecting rods sported cast aluminum alloy pistons wearing Molybdenum-inlay and chrome plated rings. A Rochester four-barrel carburetor squirted premium gasoline demanded, by the 10.25 to 1 compression wedge-head combustion chambers. The camshaft operated overhead valves via the usual pushrod rocker arm setup. The four specially tuned pace car engines carried the serial number e.g., 98168A;B.

These four 108.1-inch wheelbase cars were supplied with Turbo Hydra-Matic transmissions, sending torque to a Positraction rear axle and heavy duty suspensions.

The striking Ermine White machine was trimmed with Bright Blue lettering and custom interiors. Approximately 100 replicas were offered to the public. Chevrolet sold 25,141 Camaro convertibles.

Three-time Indy winner Mauri Rose drove the pace car. "I like to put as many bricks as I can between me and the guy chasing me," Rose had often said. He certainly proved he had lost none of his fire behind the wheel, giving the starting field a rapid sendoff.

Mr. Rose had done extensive engineering work on the Camaro's disc brake system.

1967

1967

INDIANAPOLIS MOTOR SPEEDWAY

Lucy and A.J. Foyt in Pace Car after the 1967 race credit line.

SS
U-S-A-1

Chevrolet Camaro
OFFICIAL PACE CAR
51ST ANNUAL INDIANAPOLIS 500 MILE RACE - MAY 30, 1967
SS

1967 Camaro Pace Cars

1967 Camaro Official and Festival car on main straightaway.

FORD TORINO

1968

One thing must always be said for the Ford Motor Company. Whether you are a fan of the "Dearborn gang" or not, when the boys with the blue oval on their uniforms make a commitment to a project, they never go at it halfheartedly.

In 1968, when Ford returned for their fifth trip to Indy as manufacturers of the pace car, they really brought along a winner—in every sense of the word.

Basically a top of the line Fairlane, the new Torino was destined to rewrite more than a few record books.

The slippery shape of the two-door fastback version of the line, were made to order for the high bank ovals of NASCAR. David Pearson won 20 Grand National events in a Fairlane on the way to the NASCAR championship. A.J. Foyt wheeled a Fairlane to USAC's stock car division title, and Benny Parsons did likewise in ARCA (Auto Racing Club of America) competition. It mattered little whether they were called Torino or Fairlane, (although Torino owners got a little miffed if their car was lumped into the general term) in racing trim it took an engineer to tell the difference.

All this, however, was after the fact, so to speak. No one knew the Torino would be so successful in racing, when it was selected as pace car.

Actually, it isn't any wonder the Torino owners were a little touchy. Their choice of automobile sported a new front suspension, a larger, tougher engine and all new sheet metal styling. That's about as new, as new can be!

Our two-door GT convertible was hustled along by the potent Thunderbird High Performance 427 Wedge "medium-riser" V-8. This rumbling cast iron 4.23 x 3.78 bore and stroker delivered a wheel churning 390 horsepower at 5600 rpm. The 10.9 compression ratio helped produce a back thumping 460 pounds of torque at a relatively moderate 3200 rpm. The overhead valves were operated by pushrods and rocker arms, with the latter mounted on a steel shaft, instead of a stud bolt. It is believed this engine was equipped with a hydraulic cam and lifters. It seems likely, the "perch" for the Motorcraft four-barrel carburetor, was a single-plane intake manifold. This was the best setup for optimum power in the high rpm range. The dual-plane intake was for general street use. This manifold was the tunnel-port version, with matching heads. The tunnel was actually a small tube through which the pushrod ran. This gave the fuel-air mixture an unobstructed path to the intake valves. While a forged steel crankshaft was available, the pace car probably used the stock cast iron version with five main bearings.

This was the swan song for Ford's 427 cubic inch engine. The following year, it was replaced by the 429.

A three-speed automatic took the brunt of the 427's brutal twist. Even the wide oval F70 x 14 tires had trouble handling the strong V-8's punch.

The 11.3-inch disc brakes on the front, and 10-inch drums on the rear, brought the 116-inch wheelbase machine to a safe stop.

The exterior was painted white with blue trim stripes, with the "official pace car lettering" in blue. As always, Ford never missed a chance to draw special attention to their new products. On either door, T-O-R-I-N-O was spelled out in bold capital letters, in reflective silver.

The five passenger interior sported front bucket seats done in blue leather. The convertible top boot matched the interior color scheme.

Mr. William C. Ford served as pace car driver. This marked the final time a member of the Ford family served in the capacity.

Indy Drivers Al Miller (behind wheel) and LeRoy Yarbrough getting in car prepare to take a lap in 1968 Pace Car.

OFFICIAL PACE CAR
TORINO

TORINO
OFFICIAL PACE CAR

CHEVROLET CAMARO

1969

For the second time in three years, the striking Camaro was chosen as pace car. The little machine had changed little. How could you improve on something the car buying public was purchasing in droves?

Our 1969 Camaro SS was powered by basically the same L78 396 cubic inch Turbo-Jet V-8 as its '67 predecessor. The bore and stroke as well as the internal parts were identical.

It was also equipped with power front disc brakes, power steering, Positraction rear axle, and ducted hood. The chassis was the standard 108.0-inch wheelbase.

Other features included 15-inch rally wheels, front and rear air spoiler, sports styled steering wheel, push-button radio, floor console, power convertible top, special instrumentation, custom deluxe seat, front shoulder belts and tinted glass. The interior was black and orange houndstooth.

The exterior was Ermine White with Bright Orange lettering and twin rally stripes.

Chevrolet produced 3,675 replica Camaro pace cars for the public.

Our pace car driver was 1960 Indianapolis winner Jim Rathmann. At that time, Jim was a Chevrolet dealer in Melbourne, Florida.

1969

Opening day at Indy, 1969 Camaro starts the activities.

6 COLOR
Chevrolet Camaro
OFFICIAL PACE CAR
53rd ANNUAL INDIANAPOLIS 500 MILE RACE
MAY 30, 1969

OLDSMOBILE 442

1970

"Oldsmobile is greatly honored to have the 442 chosen as the 1970 pace car for this premier automotive racing event." With these words, Mr. John B. Beltz, Oldsmobile general manager and vice president of General Motors, announced the speedway's choice as pace car.

The beautiful white convertible was powered by a 455 cubic inch overhead valve V-8 with a bore and stroke of 4.125 x 4.250. The powerful, slightly under-square five main bearing cast iron engine produced 365 horsepower at 4660 rpm. The 10.25 to 1 engine was fed by a Rochester four-barrel carburetor. Hydraulic valve lifters were employed in the conventional valve train.

The manual transmission was a fully sychronized three-speed floor-mounted heavy-duty unit, topped by a Hurst shifter. Heavy-duty suspension featured front and rear stabilizer bars to control the 112-inch wheelbase chassis' ride.

The white exterior was effectively set off by black and red striping on the hood, rear deck lid and sides of the car. The convertible top was white, while the interior was finished in jet black leather. Other special features included a fiberglass hood, functional air-induction scoops, specially painted white super stock wheels mounting wide-oval raised white letter tires.

The 442 was initially a mid-year performance car option in the 1964 Oldsmobile Cutlass line. The marque was so popular, it became a separate series in 1968.

Two-time Indianapolis 500 winner, Rodger Ward, served as pace car driver of the stylish and powerful 442.

1970

INDIANAPOLIS MOTOR SPEEDWAY

Harlan Fengler in the 1970 Oldsmobile 442 Pace Car.

Bobby Unser, 1968 winner takes a group of people for a lap around Indy in the Olds 442 (1970).

1970 Olds 442 await the arrival of the 500 Festival drivers.

DODGE CHALLENGER

It had been seventeen years since a Dodge had led the field over the starting line at Indianapolis.

In 1971, Chrysler and a group of four local Indianapolis dealerships, provided the speedway with a beautiful Challenger convertible. Since sales of the more powerful cars were in a steady decline, it was hoped the Indy exposure would revive interest in the performance car market. A backup pace car, and 50 replicas for pre-race festivities, were also supplied. Only 2165 Challenger convertibles were produced.

The striking bright "Hemi-Orange" machine, was powered by the tried and true cast iron 383 cubic inch overhead valve V-8 with a bore and stroke of 4.250 x 3.375. This hefty cast iron powerhouse pumped out 300 horsepower at 4800 rpm. The 10.0 to 1 compression pistons drew premium leaded gasoline from a four-barrel Carter carburetor, while the valves were actuated via pushrod and rocker arm. The fully counterbalanced crankshaft ran in five main bearings.

Facing mandatory pollution laws, General Motors had already drastically cut their compression ratios. Chrysler was still maintaining higher compression engines, especially in their performance cars. In light of this, the Challenger must be considered one of the few "stock" engine Indy Pace Cars in the last two decades.

A three-speed Torqueflite automatic transmission sent the power to Firestone F70 x 14 raised white letter R/T belted tires. The 110-inch wheelbase chassis utilized torsion bar suspension up front, leaf springs aft.

The interior was done in white leather, with matching convertible top and appropriate pace car lettering.

The Challenger was in every way, an example of the "muscle car" of the day. The clean design was little changed from the previous year, when Challenger had been in great evidence in drag racing.

Local Dodge dealer, Eldon Palmer, served as pace car driver, while former astronaut, John Glenn, television sportscaster Chris Schenkel and speedway owner Tony Hulman rode as passengers on the pace lap.

The Challenger went out of control on pit lane, and crashed into a photographers stand injuring some 20 people. The pace car passengers were only shaken or slightly injured.

This is the only accident involving a pace car in 500 history.

Senator Barry Goldwater on race day, 1971.

1971 Dodge Challenger leads the field on the pace lap.

55TH INDIANAPOLIS 500 MILE RACE
MAY 29, 1971
Dodge
OFFICIAL PACE CAR

HURST/OLDS CUTLASS

1972

For the second time in three years, an Oldsmobile was chosen as Indy's pace car. This was the first instance of a major automotive supplier's name—Hurst Performance Products—being included in the pace car's title.

The pace car was based on a production Cutlass convertible chassis, with a 112-inch wheelbase.

Our pace car was powered by basically the same 455 cubic inch V-8 that whistled the 1970 442 around the Brickyard. One significant change, however, was the lower 8.5 to 1 compression ratio, which whittled the big overhead valve engine down to 300 horsepower at 4700 rpm. This was necessary due to the advent of anti-pollution systems, and the debate over the coming use of unleaded gasoline. The still potent engine retained the same undersquare 4.125 x 4.250 bore and stroke as in previous years. A Rochester four-barrel carburetor breathed through a functional forced air hood, while dual exhausts with trumpet outlets scavenged off the burned gasses.

A Hurst Dual Gate shifter mounted in a center floor console, controlled the three-speed Hydra-Matic transmission.

Rallye suspension and the latest white letter Goodyear G60 x 14 Polysteel tires were mounted on Super Stock III wheels. Power disc brakes were featured on the front, while drum units brought up the rear.

The exterior was Cameo White with "Hurst Custom Laser Stripes" done in Hurst Gold. Jet Black accent stripes set off the matching leather interior.

Some 130 H/O replica convertibles and 499 Hurst/Olds coupes were offered to the public.

Former Indianapolis 500 winner, Jim Rathmann, drove our pace car.

1972

Indiana Bell
OFFICIAL PACE CAR

OFFICIAL PACE CAR
56TH ANNUAL INDIANAPOLIS 500 MILE RACE
MAY 27, 1972
GOODYEAR

CADILLAC ELDORADO

1973

When the front-wheel-drive Eldorado convertible was chosen as pace car for 1973, it marked only the second time a "puller" would lead the field. The only other front-wheel-drive pace car to that date, had been the 1930 Cord.

The convertible was making a last stand at Cadillac. A company with the reputation as one of the world's foremost producers of convertibles. New safety standards would make this one of the last "rag tops" made by Cadillac for a long time. It became a much sought after collector's item. The graceful lines of the Eldorado was certainly a favorite with the public.

Cadillac was faced with one major problem with the pace car. By '73 the large V-8 engine was carrying a much lower compression than its predecessors. This was due to emission controls, and the new non-lead gasolines just ready to come on the market. A standard Caddy V-8 was only producing 235 horsepower. While more than adequate for the highway, it wasn't enough horses to escape the accelerating 33-car field, capable of lapping the speedway at 195 mph.

Undaunted, Cadillac produced a far from stock pace car. The regular 500 cubic inch 4.30 x 4.30 square bore and stroke V-8 engine was fitted with high compression pistons. The emission controls were completely removed, as was the air conditioning. In short, everything that could sap power from the engine was removed. A custom made dual exhaust system replaced the stock single pipe factory system. The forged steel crankshaft ran in five main bearings. Up top, valves were actuated via the usual pushrod rocker arm arrangement from a single in block camshaft. A Rochester four-barrel carburetor fed fuel to the ponies. All this resulted in an engine that reportedly produced well over 500 horsepower at a modest 3800 rpm. One colt per cubic inch isn't too shabby in anyone's book!

If this figure is correct, and from all our research it appears to be, the '73 Eldorado is the most powerful pace car in Indianapolis history.

The transmission was a 3-speed Turbo Hydra-Matic. In order to assure controlled stops of the 126.3-inch wheelbase car from above 130 mph, the suspension and brakes were special heavy duty units.

Cadillac officials were reluctant to say exactly how many other modifications were made to the pacemaker. "It sure isn't 'street legal,' that's for sure," one of them was quoted as saying. One thing for sure, winner Gordon Johncock didn't receive the keys to this particulary beautiful brute!

Returning as pace car driver was Jim Rathmann, a man accustomed to leading the field at Indy.

1973

1973 Cadillacs lined up on the track.

Harlan Fengler in Cadillac

1973 Indiana Governor Otis Bowen in the Cadillac Pace Car.

HURST/OLDS CUTLASS

1974

For the second time in three years, Hurst/Olds teamed up to field the pace car. This beautiful machine, however, was far different from the 1972 Cutlass.

Since convertibles were no longer in vogue, this specially built open-roof Cutlass series car had its top removed. This modification was carried out in the Hurst plant in Detroit. A specially designed roll bar encased in black leather, to match the interior was designed for safety and styling.

Two cars, a primary and a backup, were supplied to the Indianapolis Motor Speedway for the fifty-eighth 500-mile classic.

The striking Cameo White cars trimmed in Hurst Gold and Black, were certainly attention grabbers.

A specially modified 455 cubic inch V-8 with a bore and stroke of 4.125 x 4.250 powered our pace car. In stock form, this engine produced 230 horsepower at 4000 rpm. Compression was 8.5 to 1 drawing through a Rochester 4MC four-barrel carburetor. The overhead valves were actuated via the normal pushrod and hydraulic lifter arrangement. The crankshaft was a five main bearing unit. A special heavy-duty cooling system kept it all operating.

A heavy-duty Olds Rallye suspension kit, and a beefed up Hydra-Matic transmission, with high-stall speed torque converter, topped by a Hurst Dual Gate Shifter, handled the power. Special Goodyear polyglass raised letter tires, mounted on five-spoke Super Stock aluminum wheels, put the punch on the road.

Some 380 of the Hurst/Olds, based on the Cutlass coupe, were made available to the general public. These cars carried the W-30 designation. These "replicas" were equipped with the Olds Rallye suspension, high performance 455 cubic inch engine with dual exhausts and Super Stock III 15-inch wheels. Hurst options included digital tachometer, Hurst Loc Lugs, chromed mud guards and security alarm system. A fleet of Hurst/Olds production 88 convertibles, were supplied to race officials, and members of the 500 Festival Committee.

Olds also supplied Mr. Tony Hulman with a custom handbuilt four-door Cutlass Salon, featuring swivel bucket seats.

Jim Rathmann served as pace car driver.

1974

The 1974 winning team!

OFFICIAL PACE CAR
HURST
OLDS
500 OFFICIAL
PACE 95 CAR

Chief Steward Tom Binford in the 1974 Hurst Olds W30.

BUICK CENTURY CUSTOM

1975

By 1975, the convertible was on its way out of our lives. This caused a minor problem for machines such as the Indianapolis 500 Pace Car.

Buick provided the speedway with a Century Custom coupe, with two removable roof panels. The roof work was done by Hurst Performance of shifter fame.

This striking machine, unlike most pace cars up to this time, was a one-of-a-kind vehicle. Although Buick produced 1,800 replicas for the public, they were powered by milder mannered 350 cubic inch V-8s. They were also equipped with the Hurst roof hatches and "Official Pace Car" decals.

The actual pace setter was muscled down the course by a highly modified 455 cubic inch overhead valve V-8 with a bore and stroke of 4.3125 x 3.900. A high-performance camshaft, larger valves, 10 to 1 compression heads and pistons, 2½ inch dual exhaust system, and specially calibrated Quadrajet four-barrel carburetor, helped this engine develop 325 horsepower. This was 120 more horses than the stock version of the 455. High-octane premium fuel was a must.

The suspension sported higher rate coil springs and larger stabilizer bars. The white mag wheels carried specially constructed raised white letter Goodyear tires, with General Motors' own tread design.

A durable Turbo Hydra-Matic three-speed transmission, twisting a 3.08 to 1 rear axle ratio, propelled our 112-inch wheelbase beauty.

The interior color scheme was blue with white leather bucket seats.

National advertising for the replicas sported a photo of the pace car, stating: "drive the car that led at Indy." This was underscored by: "Buick, dedicated to the Free Spirit in just about everyone."

Actor/racer James Garner drove this beautifully prepared car on race day.

Since this was basically a special car, and because of the nostalgia for the convertible, Buick supplied 40 red, white and blue LaSabre "drop tops" for use by IMS officials and members of the 500 Festival Committee.

As an added attraction, the Famous Buick "Bug" race car took a lap of honor around the track prior to the race. This car was made famous by the exploits of Louis Chevrolet and Bob Burman, who drove this type car to many victories around 1910.

1975

Bobby Unser and Dan Gurney in the 1975 Buick Free Spirit

Tom Binford poses with the '75 Buick Free Spirit

1976 Buick V-6 Free Spirit

BUICK TURBOCHARGED V-6

1976

For the first time since 1914, when Stoddard-Dayton was selected two years straight, a marque had succeeded itself as pace car at Indianapolis. This time, Buick really showed off its class—and if ever doubted—its originality.

Instead of using brute force to power their striking orange, black and grey Century, the gentlemen of Flint produced a 231 cubic inch turbocharged overhead valve V-6. It was claimed the turbocharger supplied by Rajay Industries nearly tripled the horsepower. Stock horsepower was rated at 105, but the heavily modified engine produced an amazing 306 horses. A special Rochester four-barrel to handle the turbo's thrust, special Delco ignition, special AC spark plugs, modified camshaft and improved flow cylinder heads from Kenne-Bell Enterprises added to the total performance package. The stock bore and stroke of 3.800 x 3.400 was retained. Special forged aluminum pistons, of lower compression, featuring larger ring lands, replaced the stock cast buckets. The twelve overhead valves were operated by pushrods and rocker arms.

Buick's engineers certainly did their homework on this engine. Much attention was given to the problem of throttle lag usually associated with turbocharged engines. The turbo was positioned directly over the intake manifold. This drastically reduced the distance the air-fuel mixture traveled from the carburetor to the engine. This gave the little engine a great boost in performance.

This was the first V-6 engine to power an Indy Pace Car.

The power went to the rear wheels through the same type Turbo Hydra-Matic transmission used to harness the power from 455 V-8's the previous year.

There were plenty of skeptics, who thought the car wouldn't be fast enough to accelerate away from the 33 car-field. These fears proved unfounded, however, when the beautiful creation made several trial runs of 90 mph in the north turn, to 130 mph at the pit entrance!

The tremendous power to weight ratio—not to mention the aerodynamic spoilers on the front bumper and trunk lid—certainly helped this car's performance. Buick's advanced design group, headed by Kenneth R. Baker, with able assistance from Jeff K. Lane and Thomas F. Wallace, shaved about 470 pounds from the standard Century's weight. The use of aluminum hood, trunk, fenders and other body panels as well as lighter weight body bracing, helped to make the car a rocket.

A heavy duty suspension system, with higher spring rates, heavy duty shock absorbers, larger stabilizer bars and faster ratio power steering, kept our 112-inch wheelbase charger pointed in the right direction.

The late country singer/stock car driver Marty Robbins was assigned as driver of this surprisingly fast machine.

This, too, was a special one of a kind pace car. Buick did, however—because of the exotic nature of the project—supply one backup car.

Buick supplied 1,290 replica Centurys, some (but not all) complete with Hurst hatches, in the pace car color scheme, complete with tape emblems.

This car, like the '75 Buick Century Custom pace car, is in the possession of the Sloan Museum in Flint, Michigan.

Eventually, a good deal of what Buick discovered in the development of this car, got onto the highway. The classy 1979 Buick Century Turbo Coupe, powered by the 3.8-liter turbocharged V-6, was a direct result of the '76 Indy Pace Car project.

1976

1976 Buick Turbocharged V-6 Pace Car. Pictured: Marty Robbins, Pace Car Driver.

Free Spirit
OFFICIAL PACE CAR
GOODYEAR
STEEL BELTED RADIAL
Free Spirit
BUICK

BUICK V6
Free Spirit
OFFICIAL PACE CAR
BUICK
GOODYEAR
GOODYEAR
GT RADIAL

OLDSMOBILE DELTA 88

1977

When the Indianapolis Motor Speedway chose the Oldsmobile Delta 88 as pace car, it marked a record sixth appearance for the marque to serve in such a capacity.

Oldsmobile produced a highly modified Delta 88 Royale coupe, sporting a unique removable top. The entire center section of the roof, and the rear quarter windows, comprising the removable top, were tinted glass. The rear section of the roof, contained a stylized roll bar.

The pacemaker was powered by a highly modified 403 cubic inch overhead valve V-8 with a bore and stroke of 4.351 x 3.385. Heavy duty valve springs, high performance camshaft, ported and polished cylinder heads and dual exhausts were employed to increase performance. The specially calibrated Rochester four-barrel carburetor breathed through a low restriction free-flow air filter.

The Hydra-Matic transmission was specially designed to upshift at higher rpm. The 116-inch wheelbase light-weight chassis, was carried by Goodyear's raised white-letter HR 60 wide oval steel belted radial ply tires, mounted on eight-inch wide red Super Stock wheels.

The exterior paint scheme was bright metallic silver set off by a special gloss black insert and red accent stripes.

The interior, including the reclining front bucket seats, were done in Firethorn red velour. A custom sport steering wheel kept things going straight.

Delta 88 Royale hardtop coupe pace car replicas were offered to the public, powered by the standard "street legal" version of the 403 engine. Indianapolis 500 promotional decals, and an electric sunroof were optional.

Movie star/racer, James Garner, was back for his second hitch as pace car driver. During the year, Garner drove a specially designed four-wheel-drive Cutlass in several major off-road events.

The actual pace car was donated to the Indianapolis Motor Speedway Museum. A second car paced the remaining events on the 1977 United States Auto Club Indy car schedule.

A.J. Foyt realized a racer's dream, by winning Indy's 500-miler for an unprecedented fourth time.

Unfortunately, this marked the last 500-mile race for speedway owner Tony Hulman. Mr. Hulman, who, in 1945, saved the world's greatest race course from becoming a housing development, passed away October 28, 1977. The speedway passed into the hands of Mary Fendrich Hulman, Tony's widow.

1977

INDIANAPOLIS MOTOR SPEEDWAY

Oldsmobile
OFFICIAL PACE CAR
Oldsmobile

Oldsmobile
Oldsmobile
Oldsmobile
OFFICIAL PACE CAR

1977 Olds with Chief Steward Tom Binford.

CHEVROLET CORVETTE

1978

Many people wondered when a Corvette would be named pace car for the Indy 500. The answer came in Corvette's twenty-fifth year of production. The rakish beauty Chevrolet turned out, was destined to become one of the classic pace cars of all-time.

The popular L82 small block 350 cubic inch V-8 with a bore and stroke of 4.000 x 3.480 powered this slick machine. This high performance engine—said to be showroom stock—produced 220 horsepower at 5200 rpm. A four-barrel Rochester carburetor fed unleaded fuel to the 8.9 to 1 compression grandchild of the trend setting 1955 V-8. The small block four bolt, five main bearing crankshaft, together with the forged alloy steel connecting rods, were considered bullet proof. No stronger stock production bottom end has ever been devised for a V-8.

The power went through a L82 Turbo Hydra-Matic transmission, with a specific high stall speed torque converter for increased performance.

The special two-tone paint was perhaps the most exotic yet seen on a pace car. The black area above the belt and wheel area and "hot" metallic silver on the lower portion of the body gave a startling shark-like effect. A red accent stripe extending the car's length along the belt line, separated the two colors.

Other exterior features were a front air dam, rear deck lid spoiler, polished aluminum spoke wheels with a red stripe, glass roof panels, white lettered tires and sport mirrors.

This was the first car with a one-piece body (fiberglass) to pace the 500.

The interior was done in the now legendary argent color called "Smoke." Even the driver's seat was special.

When the pace car announcement was made October 17, 1977, orders for replicas flooded the Chevrolet Motor Division offices. Initially, 2,500 replicas were to be produced at $13,653.21 per unit. The order swelled to 6,500 before race day, then an additional 500 afterwards. The sales of the so called "Limited Edition" pace car were so great, they even drew the attention of **The Wall Street Journal**. The demand continued, and a price tag of up to $28,000 was not unheard of. An article in **The New York Times** quoted an asking price of $75,000! A few counterfeit replica pace cars—complete with alloy wheels, lettering and IMS winged logo—were available. To date, it is the most sought after pace car replica.

Jim Rathmann, back for his fifth "start" as pace car driver, wheeled our beauty on race day.

In addition to the Corvette, Chevrolet provided a large number of Camaro Z28s and Monte Carlos as parade vehicles and courtesy cars for Indy 500 Festival and IMS officials. Chevrolet trucks and vans served as support vehicles during the month of May.

1978

INDIANAPOLIS MOTOR SPEEDWAY

OFFICIAL PACE CAR
corvette
CHEVROLET
USA-1
GT RADIAL

Speedway owner Tony Hulman passed away 10 days after this photo was taken.

Chief Steward Tom Binford poses with 1978 Corvette Pace Car.

FORD MUSTANG II

1979

1979

After a fifteen year absence, the Ford Mustang returned to Indy as pace car. During that interval, a great many changes had been made in the popular marque. The stylish little critter had been poked, pinched and squeezed beyond belief. When the first Mustang II appeared in 1974, it was a smart, compact machine. As the decade wore on, the "Pony II" took on a decidely "Pintoish" look. By 1979, however, the Mustang II had regained its original direction and even more stylish looks.

Our pace car was a very special machine, ushering in a new era of specialized pacemakers that would dominate the 1980s. While the engine was based on the 302 cubic inch 5.0 liter V-8 with a bore and stroke of 4.000 x 3.000, many major components were a mixture of Ford's other versatile power plants.

The cast iron block was sent to Jack Roush Performance Engineering in Lavonia, Michigan, where its deck surfaces were milled. Roush also honed the cylinder walls, and align-bored the crankshaft journals. Fully grooved Clevite 77 main bearings were used to improve oil flow to the stock cross drilled, forged steel, five main bearing Boss 302 crankshaft. All reciprocating parts, including the standard 302 rods, special TRW pistons, crankshaft, flywheel and damper, were dynamically balanced. A high performance Roush oil pump distributed the lubricant from a special seven quart oil pan. Topside, a pair of early 351 Windsor heads, featuring large ports, stock valves, stock springs and retainers from a 289 High Performance engine, were fitted to the 302 block. The heads were subjected to a .080-inch slice, which upped the compression to a staggering 10.9 to 1. The rocker arm studs were also vintage 289. Jack Roush heat-treated pushrods and guide plates took their cue from a Boss 302 camshaft and lifters. The pistons were milled .040-inch and the notch in the piston crowns were enlarged, in order to clear the larger Windsor valves. The two-plane Carroll Shelby aluminum high-rise intake manifold had to be specially machined to fit the 302 block. A four-barrel Holley carburetor took a deep breath through a chrome plated Ford Police Intercepter air cleaner. But the deep breathing didn't stop there. A sport-tuned exhaust system, without a catalytic converter, kept restrictions to a minimum. All this modification produced some 280 horsepower, a gain of some 141 mighty thoroughbreds over the stock Mustang II 302 engine. You could say, our Pony turned into a Horse!

A modified Ford C-4 Select-Shift automatic transmission, with high-stall-speed torque converter and external transmission fluid cooler, took the kick.

The front disc brakes were Fairmont Police units, using semi-metallic linings. The rear snubbers were stock drum units.

The front suspension utilized struts with coil springs on the lower A-arms, and a front-mounted stabilizer bar to control roll. The rear axle was controlled by a four-bar link setup, with coil springs and shock absorbers mounted outside the frame rails. This gave the 100.4-inch wheelbase Pony a surprisingly stable ride.

The pace car was often photographed shod with special Michelin blackwall 190/65R390 TRX tires, mounted on Michelin's 150 TR 390 forged-aluminum three-spoke wheels. The combination was so successful, Michelin patented the wheels and tires as a unit.

On race day, however, the actual pace car was wearing Goodyear tires. Ford entered into a development program with Goodyear just prior to Indy. From the results of this undertaking, Goodyear produced the new "Wing Foot" tire for highway use.

The exterior finish, consisting of six coats of pewter paint and four coats of clear acrylic lacquer, was contrasted with flat black trim. The racy machine carried red and orange "Official Pace Car" lettering. The well known running Mustang logo, in multi-exposure, adorned each front fender. A special non-production T-top, from Cars and Concepts of Brighton, Michigan, added even more character to the already sporty vehicle. The design team, headed up by Jack Telnack, based the Mustang II around the three-door notchback body style. A special front air dam, rear aerodynamic spoiler, horizontal-bar grille and simulated rear opening hood scoop were the products of the Ford Design Center. To further improve aerodynamics, the chassis was lowered one-inch. The result was a drag coefficient of only .44.

Special adjustable Recaro bucket seats, upholstered with black and white cloth inserts and trimmed in black cloth and vinyl, added a striking appearance to the interior. A console mounted floor shift, was also featured.

Ford produced 11,000 replicas, which appeared as a mid-year addition to the little Pony's line. This was probably the largest reproduction of Indy Pace Cars in history, and its popularity resulted in the Cobra design for 1980.

Ford actually produced three of the special pace cars. Cars number two and three escorted the actual pacemaker on the parade lap, pitting after the initial circuit. "One of the most exciting" experiences in my life was to be fortunate enough to drive the number two pace car on that lap," Mr. Glen S. Lyall, who still works at Ford's Experimental Vehicle Division, informed this writer.

Three-time World Driving Champion, Jackie Stewart, who was certainly no stranger to speed, drove the pace car. It must be noted that Stewart was leading the 1966 Indianapolis 500 at 190 laps, when his oil pressure failed, allowing Graham Hill to win. So far as we are able to ascertain, Stewart is the only foreign pace car driver in Indy history.

LONI ANDERS
WKRP IN CINCINNA
OFFICIAL PACE C

Stewards Art Myers and Keith Ward of USAC with the 1979 Mustang.

PONTIAC TURBO-TRANS AM

1980

1980

To say the white 1980 Trans Am pace car was stunning, was quite an understatement. Trimmed out in charcoal and red striping, with distinctive "fire-breathing" hood decal, this silky smooth machine drew attention wherever it went.

Pontiac made the most of the Indianapolis publicity. It was difficult to miss seeing an advertisment for the Trans Am in magazines, newspapers or on television.

Our beauty was powered by a 4.9-liter 301 cubic inch turbocharged V-8 with a bore and stroke of 4.000 x 3.000. The compression ratio on the turbo was 7.5 to 1, producing 210 horsepower at 4000 rpm. The crankshaft ran in five main bearings, and the overhead valves were actuated via pushrod and rocker arms. Fuel was metered by a Rochester four-barrel carburetor. A three-speed Hydra-Matic transmission handled the torque, sending the power to a 3.08 limited-slip rear axle. Disc brakes were standard on all four wheels, bringing the 108.2-inch wheelbase chassis to a sure stop.

Silver tinted removable hatch roofs were standard on the pace car. A hood mounted turbo-boost gauge faced the driver. The over-all sporty appearance of the Trans Am was enhanced even further by 15-inch white aluminum "air-flow" wheels mounting Goodyear 225/70R15 white letter tires.

The interior sported Oyster Vinyl bucket seats with black Hobnail Cloth inserts, power windows and custom seat belts. Embroidered Bird designs adorned the door pads, and the rear seat center. A leather encased steering wheel guided our beautiful beast, while Soft-Ray Glass in all windows, protected passengers from the sun. Red instrument panel lighting made the vital signs easy to read.

This was one of the least modified pace cars since the early 1970s. In fact, Pontiac officials often claimed the biggest modification was the removal of the air conditioning system.

Mr. John Schinella, chief designer at Pontiac Exterior Two Studio, was responsible for the over-all design.

Some 6,300 4.9-liter Trans Ams were produced. However, the special Indianapolis 500 pace car decals had to be ordered through Pontiac dealerships.

The late Johnnie Parsons, Sr., Indianapolis winner in 1950, was our pace car driver, and enjoyed himself tremendously.

1980 Pace Car driver, Johnnie Parsons, 1950 winner of the 500 poses with Trans Am Pace Car.

PONTIAC
OFFICIAL PACE CAR
TURBO-TRANS AM
64th ANNUAL INDIANAPOLIS 500 MILE RACE
MAY 25, 1980
TRANS AM
GOODYEAR

1980 Trans Am Pontiac Pace Car with driver Johnnie Parsons and his 1950 Indy winning Wynns SPL.

BUICK REGAL

1981

When it was announced that Buick would be the 1981 Indy Pace Car, everyone, remembering the exotic 1976 offering, waited to see what it would produce. The result was well worth the wait.

A "very special" Regal, designed at Lloyd E. Ruess' Special Products Engineering, under the guiding hand of Herbert A. Fishel, arrived for inspection. The beautiful paint scheme, silver with dark maroon "Maple" trim and orange stripes, really got the attention of racing fans.

The roof of the two-door Regal was completely cut away, replaced by a leather covered roll bar, with a brace running from the windshield frame for added strength and rigidity. This 108.1-inch wheelbase beauty was a true parade car, with occupants encumbered by hatch roofs.

Nestled under the hood was a 4.1-liter (252 cubic inch) overhead valve V-6 with a bore and stroke of 3.965 x 3.400. The muscular 12.5 to 1 compression ratio, was one of the highest figures in pace car history. This potent engine delivered 281 horsepower at 5100 rpm. This was an increase of 156 ponies over the stock version of the same engine. Wringing such horsepower from so small a normally aspirated engine—especially a pushrod job—was quite a feat. This special engine was the work of Buick engineers and Baker Engineering of Grand Rapids, Michigan.

Obviously, there was a great amount of modification done to this engine. No doubt, a special cam, larger valves, special heads, higher compression pistons, etcetera, entered into it. Much of the exact information on this engine is still under wraps.

The stock version of this engine was standard fare for the Riviera and Electra, as well as being optional for the LaSabre.

Once again, the reliable Turbo Hydra-Matic spun the gold lace alloy wheels.

The interior colors complimented the exterior striping. Special Recaro seats done in orange, gold and maple leather, matched the padded "patchwork" door panels.

Duke Nalon, the master of the Novi, was the pace car driver and enjoyed every moment of it.

This particular car was unique in another respect. It was also the pace car for the July 4, 1981 Pike's Peak Hill Climb.

1981

BUICK
BUICK
INDIANAPOLIS
500

GOODYEAR
EAGLE GT

OFFICIAL PACE CAR
65TH
INDIANAPOLIS

Indy Novi Driver of the '40's and '50's Duke Nalon drove the 1981 Buick Pace Car.

CHEVROLET CAMARO Z28

1982

For the third time since 1967, a Chevrolet Camaro was chosen as pace car. This was the marque's fifteenth year of production.

This particular Camaro, with Vehicle Identification Number 1G1AP8772CL100887, was the first Z28 built at GM's Van Nuys, California facility. Shipped to the Chevrolet Engineering Center in Warren, Michigan, it underwent extensive modifications.

Our pace car was powered by a hybrid small block V-8. The 350 cubic inch engine retained the stock bore and stroke measurements of 4.000 x 3.480. There, all similarity to a stock engine ended. The cylinder block was cast aluminum heavy duty 356 alloy with cast iron liners and four-bolt main caps. The heads were aluminum, too, with 2.02 intake and 1.62-inch exhaust valves. The camshaft was the famous high speed-high, high-lift camshaft version designed for the mid-1960s Corvette. Hydraulic valve lifters operated the usual pushrod, rocker arm arrangement. The 11.1 compression forged aluminum pistons were fitted to heavy duty LT-1 connecting rods. The crankshaft was heavyduty, heat treated, forged steel. A "Cross-Fire" electronic fuel injection unit, utilizing twin throttle-bodies, sat atop an aluminum crossflow tuned intake manifold. Injector and manifold were stock Z28 equipment. Stainless steel 1½-inch headers, feeding into 2¾-inch pipe and twin low-restriction mufflers, scavenged off exhaust gases. A stock electronic ignition system, with 38-degrees total advance, lit everything off. All this effort produced 250 horsepower at a conservative 4600 rpm.

The engine project was under the direction of Vince Piggins, Chevrolet's veteran product performance manager. "What we had was a cross between the full-race stock-block Chevy found in some Indianapolis racing machines, and the stock 5.0-liter 1982 Z28 engine," observed Mr. Piggins.

A three-speed Turbo Hydro-Matic transmission turned 15-inch aluminum wheels, mounting P245/60R Goodyear Eagle GT blackwalls. A stock suspension system incorporating stabilizer bars fore and aft, high-rate coil springs, modified MacPherson struts in front and a torque arm with Panhard rod in the rear, helped put the ponies on the ground. Four-wheel disc brakes brought things to a stop.

The exterior was a unique silver and blue, while the interior sported six-way adjustable seats of dark blue cloth with silver vinyl trim and sewn-in Z28 logo. Special instruments, including a 140 mph speedometer, filled the dash. Removable glass roof panels were a feature.

A backup pace car was built in January '82. Some 6,000 "Commemorative Edition" Z28s, with stock engines, were offered to the public.

Jim Rathmann, back for his sixth time as pace car driver, guided the spirited machine. Thus Jim equaled Sam Hanks' record for most years as pace car driver.

1982

INDIANAPOLIS MOTOR SPEEDWAY

1982 Camaro during a track inspection by Steward Keith Ward.

INDIANAPOLIS
500

INDIANAPOLIS
500
3

BUICK RIVIERA

1983

Riviera has always meant class, and the beautifully crafted 1983 pace car was no exception. By this time, Buick had returned to the long lamented convertible. The clean, artful lines of the Riviera were the work of designer Bill Porter.

The pace car was cream, trimmed in light chocolate brown.

The interior was richly turned out with real wood panels and wood steering wheel.

The 4.1-liter (252 cubic inch) overhead valve V-6 engine was a masterful blend of engineering art and the very latest high-tech achievements. The only thing stock about this engine was the 3.965 x 3.400 bore and stroke measurements. A specially designed twin-turbocharger arrangement gave our beauty a 450 horsepower kick. The turbos were highly modified production units. All major functions were controlled by a Delco Electronics computer. This included ignition, idle speed, air-fuel mixture and turbocharger wastegate. In short, just about everything—except pace car driver Duke Nalon's right foot.

The engine was said to be the most technically advanced power plant to orbit the speedway, up to that time. Even the potent racing engines took a back seat to this advanced piece of Flint Michigan's finest art.

With the hood opened or closed, this was one of the most photographed Indy Pace Cars in history.

The elegant 114-inch wheelbase machine was pulled by front-wheel-drive.

Duke was certainly partial to this goin' machine.

"It was a beautiful car to drive and reminded me of the Novi," Duke said. "Also, it was front-drive which I enjoyed driving during my days in the 500."

All we can add is, he sure looked natural wheeling a cream-colored streak off the north turn.

In 1983, Buick enjoyed its largest sales year, up to that time. Some 810,435 units were sold.

The Buick V-6 continued to advance.

In 1984, the design was the basis for the turbocharged Buick V-6 Indy racing engines, used by Scott Brayton and Pat Bedard.

During time trials for the 1985 Indy 500, Pancho Carter won the pole position, wheeling a Buick V-6 to a new track record of 212.583 mph. Brayton put his Buick right along side Carter on the front row, with a blistering single lap record of 214.199.

Since then, the little engines have been constant contenders at Indy.

Most recently, a Buick V-6 Lola carried Jim Crawford to a convincing sixth finish in the 1988 Indy classic. Crawford led at the half way point, and remained in contention for most of the race. A last minute pit stop, caused by a tire problem, cost him a real chance at victory.

There is little doubt that Buick's racing success is tied directly to its efforts with the Indy Pace Cars.

1983

Official Pace Car
67th INDIANAPOLIS 500 · MAY 29, 1983

BUICK
500

PONTIAC FIERO

1984

The 1984 Indianapolis 500 was paced by the revolutionary, space-age, mid-engined Pontiac Fiero. The smooth little machine was so outstanding in concept and design, it came to the attention of Indianapolis Motor Speedway officials in its first production year.

Our pace car was powered by an aftermarket Super Duty 2.7-liter 4-cylinder, stabling 232 horses at 6500 rpm. This 165 cubic inch stormer, bristling with aftermarket goodies, possessed a bore and stroke of 3.500 x 3.000. A beefier engine block, forged steel fully counterbalance crankshaft and special high performance head helped boost the engine output. Throttle body fuel injection served up the juice. The pace car air intake was relocated lower in the front fascia, providing better air flow. A four tube header and low resonation dual outlet exhaust system scavenged the burned gases.

Even the engine's outer appearance was given attention, with silver painted rocker arm cover, air cleaner, stainless steel oil filler cap and red spark plug wiring. A special heavy duty four-speed transmission put the power on the road. Higher rear spring rates, along with Delco/Bilstein high pressure shock absorbers, handled the bumps. Delco electric power-master vented disc brakes dropped the hook. The actual pace car rode on high-tech polished aluminum wheels, mounting Goodyear Eagle GT tires.

The greatest engineering feature of the Fiero, was the "space frame chassis". Fiero was the first production car in the world to utilize the concept. The sheet metal front compartment sub-assembly, rear engine compartment, body sides, roof and floor pan were all welded together to form the chassis. Galvanized and high strength steel was also utilized.

Twenty-six Unimate robot welders made the 4,300 plus spot welds required. The entire bare chassis weighed a mere 600 pounds, with a wheelbase of only 93.4-inches. The latter figure makes the Fiero the smallest Indy pace car in history.

A procedure called "mill-and-drill" machined the space frame to precise tolerances, insuring a pefect fit with the sleek body.

One of the major applications of leading edge technology was the use of a space-age body material called "Enduraflex." This was a reinfoced composition material—the basis of which was polyeurethane—that returned to its original shape after minor impact. Approximately 100 pounds of sheet molded compound (SMI) was used for the roof, rear deck lid, hood and upper rear quarter panels. Heavier reinforced reaction injection molding (RRIM) was used for door panels, front fenders, sides of the car and lower rear quarter panels.

A more flexible RRIM was used on the almost unnoticable front bumper fascias, while RIM finds the same use at the rear. Chip and dent resistant Thermo Plastic Olefin formed the rocker panels.

The pace car was painted white with a silver lower accent and red trim stripe. Light grey leather seats with red cloth inserts filled the cockpit, which was equipped with a removable sunroof.

Aerodynamically, the Fiero was as clean as any aircraft. Side and rear skirts and a functional rear-deck wing, contributed to positive handling and ground effects of the car. Even the rear high-intensity strobe safety light was integrated into the back edge of the air scoop. The lighting system was adapted from a Boeing 747.

Pontiac produced 2,000 replica pace cars for the market, powered by the standard 2.5-liter engine.

This was the first 4-cylinder engine to pace Indy, since before World War I. If there was any skepticism about the four-banger producing sufficient escape speed, they were all put to rest when the Fiero turned a lap of the Brickyard at better than 136 mph!

Mr. John G. Callies, manager of the Motorsports Engineering Division of Pontiac, served as pace car driver.

As amazing as the Fiero project was, the marque was dropped from the Pontiac line during 1988. This should make these cars very valuable in years to come, and the Indy pace car replicas, even more so.

1984

1984 Fiero with TV Star David Hasselhoff of Knight Rider.

Indy Fiero

1984 Pontiac Fiero with Pace Car driver/Engineer John Callies during testing session.

OLDS CALAIS

1985

For the first time in its history as 500-mile race pace car, Oldsmobile took to the track with less than eight cylinders.

The highly modified car, designated the Calais 500, was powered by a special 2.7-liter 4-cylinder engine. The potent 165 cubic inch L-4 motor, possessing a bore and stroke of 3.500 x 3.000, was derived from the standard Calais powerplant, delivering 215 horsepower at 6500 rpm. Highly refined cylinder head, block and crankshaft were produced for the Calais 500. Custom made pistons and special high life long duration camshaft, were part of the performance package. The 9.5 to 1 compression made the use of premium unleaded fuel a necessity. An electronic control module (ECM) controlled the base air/fuel mixture, acceleration fuel enrichment and deceleration fuel cutoff. The ECM also monitored a number of other functions, including throttle position and RPM.

To handle the more than double stock horsepower output, a special engine mounting system utilizing urethane bushings, as opposed to stock rubber mounts, had to be fabricated.

The front-wheel-drive was linked to the engine via a special three-speed transmission, with a torque converter clutch for the third gear. A firm shift calibration package, high capacity band and five-plate direct clutch were incorporated. The turbine shaft was forged steel, and the chain sprockets were heavy duty units.

Handling was enhanced by 30 percent stiffer than stock springs. The body was also lowered one-inch all around. Special shocks were revalved to be 100 percent stiffer in jounce and 150 percent stiffer in rebound. The mounting bushings were made from solid moly-impregnated nylon. The rubber met the track on special 16 x 7 racing wheels mounting V225/50R16 low profile tires.

The actual pace car was a one of a kind "open roofed" four-passenger model Calais. The special Fiesta red metallic finish, was highlighted by silver leather seats and interior trim. A removable rollbar and competition style seat belts and shoulder harness were installed on the actual pace car. The pacer lighting system was housed in an integral, trunk-mounted rear spoiler.

A limited coupe version of the Indy pace car was offered to the public through Oldsmobile dealerships.
Popular James Garner returned as pace car driver. A position he had filled twice before in 1975 and '77.

1985

INDIANAPOLIS MOTOR SPEEDWAY

James Garner driving the Pace Car.

OFFICIAL PACE CAR
69TH INDIANAPOLIS 500 · MAY 26, 1985
AL UNSER, JR. 7 COORS LIGHT SILVER BULLET
TEO FABI 33 FORSYTHE RACING SKOAL BANDIT
CHIP GANASSI 40 OLD MILWAUKEE BEER
GORDON JOHNCOCK 20

CHEVROLET CORVETTE

1986

"Chevrolet is back in Indianapolis in 1986 because of what Chevrolet and the 500 mean—competition, teamwork, winning and, most of all, automobiles." With these words, Mr. Robert D. Burger, Chevrolet general manager and a General Motors vice-president, announced Corvette as the pace car. The pace car image was enhanced, when Corvette's Bowling Green, Kentucky plant turned out the first 'Vette convertible in fifteen years.

Our bright yellow 'Vette roadster, one of the few stock production cars to pace the 500 in the 1980s, was powered by the tried and true 5.7-Liter V-8. The faithful 350 cubic incher with a bore and stroke of 4.000 x 3.480 and Tuned Port Injection, pumped out 230 horsepower at 4000 rpm. An electric in-tank, positive-displacement rollervane fuel pump supplied the gas. The usual tough Chevy bottom end, cam and valve train assembly were employed. A Computer Command Control watched over the whole thing.

The transmission was a four-speed manual with computer controlled overdrive in second through fourth gears and a high-stall torque converter. The fully independent four-wheel suspension was controlled by monoleaf glass-expoxy composite transverse springs fore and aft. Forged aluminum suspension arms controlled the sway on both ends. New heavy duty Bosch designed anti-lock disc brakes stopped all four wheels.

All soft top '86 Corvettes, no matter what their color, were considered pace car replicas. These roadsters are designated Z51.

The pace car driver was as big a drawing card as the 'Vette itself. United States Air Force Brigadier General, retired, Chuck Yeager—the guy with "The Right Stuff"—who first shattered the sound barrier as an Air Force test pilot, led the field to the flag. A personable, friendly man, "General Chuck" is certainly one of the most popular pace car drivers in Indy history.

1986

1986 Corvette with winner Bobby Rahal, wife Debbi and car owner Jim Trueman.

CORVETTE
OFFICIAL PACE CAR
70TH INDIANAPOLIS 500·MAY 25,1986

CHEVROLET
CHALLENGER
Bud
OFFICIAL PACE CAR

CHRSYLER LeBARON

1987

1987

The choice of Chrysler as 1987 pace car, marked the end of a twenty-four year Indy drought for MoPar's top line marque. And what a way to end a drought!

"Storming" down the front stretch on race day, was the outstandingly handsome LeBaron convertible. This sleek "real" convertible was powered by a 4-cylinder of 2.2-liters (135 cubic inches) with a bore and stroke of 3.44 x 3.62 inches. The cast iron engine made use of an aluminum head, with belt-driven single overhead camshaft operating hydraulic lifters. A Decca-Bendix fuel-injector unit replacing the stock Bosch setup, was teamed with Chrysler's multi-point fuel delivery system. The AiResearch TO 3 turbocharger pumped 12.0 pounds of boost into the 8.1 to 1 compression engine. The use of special 108-octane gasoline allowed an advance in ignition timing, and a change in the electronic control logic module. A 2½ inch exhaust system replaced the stock counterpart, allowing for better breathing and top end acceleration. The pistons, connecting rods and five main bearing crankshaft were stock units. All this produced 230 horsepower at something in the vacinity of 5200 rpm. These ponies were ample enough to haul the LeBaron into the 140-150 mph range.

The front-wheel-drive received the power from a five-speed manual transmission, utilizing equal length half shafts to overcome torque steer.

The LeBaron was marketed as a luxury sports coupe or convertible, not a performance car. This in mind, the pace car was equipped with a factory option suspension that included high control gas-charged struts, shock absorbers and heavy duty front and rear sway bars. Front coil spring rates were increased from 85 pounds per inch to 120, while the rear coils went from 160 to 200. Special harder bushings were used on the lower control arms. The rack and pinion power-assisted steering was quickened from the standard 14 to 1 ratio to 16 to 1.

The standard braking system was replaced by a Chrysler four-wheel power disc setup. The 100.3-inch wheelbase beauty was shod with blackwall P225/50VR15 Goodyear tires, mounted on 6 x 15 inch cast aluminum road wheels.

Since the LeBaron was designed from the ground up as a convertible—unlike many recent pace cars—it required no special structural supports to retain body rigidity.

The bright red exterior sported hideaway headlights that simply disappeared into the slick swept-back styling.

This was effectively set off by black leather interior. Appointments included digital speedometer, fuel gauge, tach and tilt-back front seats.

Safety equipment consisted of the strobe light system, hand fire extinguishers in the passenger compartment and a manual underhood Halon extinguisher unit. Pyro Tech designed a special occupant restraint, featuring V-shaped shoulder belts combined with a unique toggle buckle fitted to a conventional lap belt.

Our pace car driver was long-time sports car competitor Carroll Shelby.

Honored with **Sports Illustrated's** 1956 and '57 "Sports Car Driver of the Year" award, and similar recognition by **The New York Times** in '58, Shelby is perhaps best remembered as the force behind the potent Shelby AC cobras. Shelby managed teams of Ford GT 40 sports cars, won at Le Mans in 1966 and '67.

In '82, the personable Texas native became associated with Crysler's performance development program. Since then, a steady stream of turbocharged, front-wheel-drive performance cars have emerged from his Chrysler-Shelby Performance Center based in Santa Fe Springs, California.

Al Unser, Sr. roared from twentieth starting position, to win his fourth Indianapolis 500-mile race. This put "Big Al" into a segment of racing's elite. Previously, only A.J. Foyt had won the Indy classic four times.

At last report, Unser still owned all four of his Indy Pace Cars.

INDIANAPOLIS MOTOR SPEEDWAY

Cum mins
CHRYSLER

CHRYSLER
OFFICIAL PACE CAR

CUTLASS SUPREME

1988

For an unprecedented eighth time, Oldsmobile was selected as Indy 500 Pace Car. It isn't difficult to understand why. From August of 1987, until just prior to the month of May, Olds was on the move—and that's putting it mildly!

The quad 4 engine, which powered the production 1988 Cutlass Calais, carried A.J. Foyt to a pair of international speed records. A.J.'s Aerotech streamliner, based on a 1985 March chassis, appeared to be right out of the space age—perhaps Indy's future.

On August 27, 1987, at the former Firestone 7.7 mile test facility near Fort Stockton, Texas, Foyt set a new world closed-course speed record of 257.123 mph. A.J. established this stunning mark at the wheel of a single turbocharged Quad 4 Aerotech ST (short tail) test car. At the same test session, "Super Tex" wheeled a twin turbocharged Quad 4 Aerotech LT (long tail) vehicle to a new world flying mile mark of 267.399.

In addition, seven major NASCAR racing teams were using the Cutlass Supreme on the Winston Cup circuit.

The special open roof Cutlass Supreme pace car, was powered by basically the same engine design as A.J.'s record smashers. The Quad 4 displaced 2.3-liters (138 cubic inches) with a bore and stroke of 3.62 x 3.35. This was just about the only stock dimension connected with this powerful engine, which developed 250 horsepower at 6000 rpm. The busy 16-valves—two exhaust, two intake—canted at a 42-degree angle in the pent-roof combustion chamber—were set in motion by double overhead camshafts and direct acting hydraulic lifters. The cams, in turn, were driven by dual timing chains. Premium unleaded fuel was conducted to the 8.8 to 1 compression engine via fuel injection and a 7.5 pound boost turbocharger, featuring a water heated throttle body and air to air intercooler. Downstairs, were special forged pistons and crankshaft, the latter running in five computer sized main bearings. The cams and rod bearings were also given computer treatment to insure low friction. All these goodies lived together in a special compact, lightweight, low-friction engine block.

The Quad 4 design represented eight years of work by Oldsmobile, and is now assigned to the Lansing Buick-Oldsmobile-Cadillac Group Powertrain organization.

The 107.5-inch wheelbase, front-wheel-drive machine delivered its power to the track through a THM 125-C three-speed Turbo Hydra-Matic transaxle with a final drive of 3.33.

The one-piece cast aluminum styled wheels and Goodyear Eagle P225/50ZR16 tires, were held to the track by Oldsmobile's FE3 handling package. This unit consisted of heavy duty swaybars, shock absorbers and struts. Incidentally, the Goodyears were speed rated at 149-plus mph.

Everything came to a safe stop when the four-wheel disc GM Delco Moraine ABS III brakes were applied. This state of the art antilock system was coupled with wheel speed sensors, a controller, hydraulic booster modulator and interconnect wiring that minimized impending wheel lockup.

Safety equipment included the by now familiar fore and aft strobe lights, 22-gallon fuel cell with dual pumps, Halon fire extinguisher system with separate outlets for underhood, fuel system area and passenger compartment. A four-point seat belt system, and detachable roll bar was also installed.

Aerodynamics also helped stick the Cutlass to the track. The lower air dam and rocker panels were improved by wind tunnel testing, resulting in more downforce for better traction and stability. An unbelievable .30 drag coefficient was attained.

Ed Magner, Olds project engineer for the pace car, reported a speed of well over 140 mph. To paraphrase the advertising slogan: "This is not your father's Oldsmobile!"

While most of the latter day pace cars have been painted white or bright colors, Oldsmobile's design studio decided to break with tradition.

1988

INDIANAPOLIS MOTOR SPEEDWAY

"When we designed the original International Series Cutlass Supreme, we painted the fiberglass model black and give it a grey lower body," said Dave North, chief designer at Oldsmobile's Exterior Studio II. "It gave the car a mysterious look that really caught your eye." And that's exactly how and what our pace car was. A beautiful black-metallic trimmed in silver-grey eye catcher!

Meanwhile, the Olds Interior Design Studio, under Larry Wallen, produced appointments just as striking as the exterior. The all leather black seats were trimmed with red piping, and embossed with the official Indianapolis Motor Speedway symbol for added character.

Instrumentation included a 7000 rpm tachometer, redlined at 6500, a 140 mph speedometer, mechanical oil pressure gauge and turbo booster monitor. A sophisticated Head Up Display (HUD) that revealed key driving data to the driver, including speed, low fuel warning, high beam and turn signal information, was something new for a pace car. The display appeared above the car's hood and in front of the windshield, so the driver need not divert his attention from the track. The HUD unit was similar to systems used in many of today's latest fighter aircraft.

All this technology must have made our pace car driver feel right at home. Popular test pilot, General Chuck Yeager, returned to Indy for his second "tour of duty."

Oldsmobile also supplied a backup pace car, and 50 Cutlass convertible parade cars equipped with folding soft tops.

1988 Olds Cutlass Supreme and pace car driver General Chuck Yeager.

Quad 4, engine of the 1988 Olds Cutlass Supreme.

1988 Olds Cutlass Supreme shown with the Olds Aerotech and the 1949 Olds 88 Pace Car.

PONTIAC TRANS AM

1989

The very latest version of the Indy Pace Car is the beautiful Pontiac Trans Am GTA. This marks the third time for Pontiac to be so honored since 1980. It is also the Twentieth Anniversary of the Pontiac Trans Am line.

Most amazing of all, this powerful "muscle car" need not be altered or modified to pace the fastest 33 racers in the world. The addition of the strobe light system is the only difference between our pacemaker and a showroom Trans Am.

"When the Trans Am paced this event in 1980, we modified the car to meet track requirements by simply leaving off the air conditioning package," recalled Pontiac general manager and General Motors vice president, J. Michael Losh. "Now we have achieved the ultimate Trans Am to date with this Twentieth Anniversary Indianapolis 500 Pace Car. A completely stock car to pace these powerful racing machines!"

Our sensational looking GTA, equipped with removable hatch roof, is powered by Pontiac's potent turbocharged 3.8-liter V-6 (231 cubic inches) with a slightly oversquare bore and stroke of 3.80 x 3.40. A cross drilled crankshaft, specific pistons and healthy 8.0 to 1 compression heads make up the essential components of this reliable engine. The overhead valves are actuated by the usual pushrod and rocker arm assembly. The unleaded gasoline is transferred via electronic port-injection, with a strong 16.5 pound assist from the intercooled turbo. All this translates to 250 horsepower at a surprisingly sedate—for this day and age—4000 rpm. Tests have shown the Trans Am to be just as quick as it looks. A speed in excess of 150 mph is within our pace car's capability. This machine certainly lives up to Pontiac's current slogan: "We Build Excitement."

The GTA puts the torque on the track with an impressively smooth THM 200R4 four-speed automatic transmission and a limited-slip differential.

Up front, the firm WS6 suspension system, consisting of MacPherson struts utilizing the new deflected-disc gas-pressurized units and coil springs, keep the nose where it belongs. Gas-pressurized shock absorbers and coil springs dampen the live rear axle, which is located by trailing arms and Panhard rod. Anti-roll bars of 36 and 24mm, front and rear, respectively, keep everything level. The 101-inch wheelbase machine is brought to a stop by vaccum assisted four-wheel disc brakes.

The sleek exterior is done in monotone Trans Am white. The cast alloy 8-inch wide gold lace wheels carry Goodyear Eagle P245/50ZR-16 blackwall tires. Split tail pipes add a touch of class to this alluring automobile.

The leather interior, including the fully articulating bucket seats, is done in Camel tan.

Pontiac will produce 1,500 replicas for the public, priced at about $28,500 per copy. All replicas will be fitted with the special Indianapolis Motor Speedway logo in cloisonne emblem form attached to the right and left rocker panel ahead of the doors. Each vehicle owner will also receive a complete set of official Indianapolis 500 Pace Car decals for the door and windshield, exactly like our seventy-third pacemaker. The GTA script on the front fenders will be replaced by a Turbo Trans Am emblem. The GTA nose emblem will be replaced by a Twentieth Anniversary insignia. Pontiac management likes to point out that "The Only Modification The T/A Needed To Pace The Indy 500 Was A Decal".

Well, as advanced and potent as the T/A is, it still needed a driver. So, 3 time Indy 500 winner Bobby Unser was assigned the driving privilege on race day.

1989

INDIANAPOLIS MOTOR SPEEDWAY

INDIANAPOLIS MOTOR SPEEDWAY
RACING CAPITAL OF THE WORLD
HALL OF FAME
PONTIAC
TURBO
OFFICIAL PACE CAR
73RD INDIANAPOLIS 500 MAY 28 1989

OFFICIAL PACE CAR

White Hot
&
Pacing the Industry
1989 PONTIAC TURBO TRANS AM
Official Pace Car of the 73rd Indy 500
10199

Mickey Mouse with the 1989 Pontiac Trans Am Pace Car.

PHOTOS WE THOUGHT YOU'D LIKE TO SEE...

Start of the 1911 500.

OFFICIAL
1941 PACEMAKER
INDIANAPOLIS
500 MILE SWEEPSTAKES
CHRYSLER

OFFICIAL
PACE CAR
OLDSMOBILE "88"

Clark Gable, Benson Ford and Wilbur Shaw in the 1950 Mercury.

Barney Oldfield in the 1920 Marmon V-16 Pace Car.

NOT QUITE THE END...

OFFICIAL CARS of the EARLY YEARS

924 Official Car (Lincoln)

1926 Official Car

1929 Official Car (Packard)

1929 Official Car (Studebaker President)

1930 Official Car (Cadillac V-6)

1931 Official Cars (Studebaker)

1932 Official Cars (Ford) Car on left: Driver, Eddie Rickenbacker; passenger, T.E. "Pop" Myers.

1933 Official Car (Oldsmobile) with Eddie Rickenbacker

1933 Official Car (DeSoto)

1933 Official Car (Rolls Royce)

1934 Official Car (Chrysler Airflow)

Seth Klein and the 1935 Official Car (Ford)

Eddie Rickenbacker and the 1937 Official Car (Pontiac 6)

1950 Official Car (Mercury) with Champion Spark Plug Man

1952 Official Car (Studebaker)

1954 Official Car (Dodge) with Martin and Lewis aboard.

1957 Official Car (Mercury), Frank Bain driver.

1990 Pace Car

1990 Pace Car

1991 Pace Car

1991 Pace Car

1992 Pace Car

1992 Pace Car

1993 Pace Car